# History On Two Needles

# History on Two Needles

Library of Congress Control Number: 2012950982

ISBN 13: 978-1-937513-18-4

First Edition

Published by Cooperative Press

http://www.cooperativepress.com

Patterns © 2012, Annie Modesitt

Photos © 2012, Jen Simonson, Annie Modesitt as noted

Models: Ellis Norris, Hannah Landy, Lisa Genis, Debra Schlekewy, Lisa Pannell, Kristen Klemmen & London Nelson

## For Cooperative Press

Senior Editor: Shannon Okey

Assistant Editor: Elizabeth Green Musselman

Technical Editor: Kate Atherley

**An iron fence in Stirling, Scotland**

*"To David Hoyle, wherever he may be, in appreciation of New Years 1987"*

*— Patti Skinner*

**Stirling Bridge, Scotland**

# Pattern Contents

# Charts

# Schematics

# A Labor of Love

For years I dreamed about a collection of designs based on iconic works from art history, blending several of my great loves (knitting, history, and art) into one set of finished patterns that anyone could knit and wear.

I wanted to create garments inspired by historic *images*, without becoming historic **costumes**. My love of historic garment silhouette, detail, and the lessons these teach us about political changes in the world is something I like to bring to my hand-knit designs whenever possible.

### MY OWN HISTORY

My master's degree is in Costume & Set Design *(I call it my "$20,000 degree in folding")*. Earning that degree at Rutgers University allowed me to indulge my great love of history and clothing and to hone the craft of telling a story through style.

After working as an Assistant Designer and Milliner on Broadway, I designed a bit off Broadway. Costuming introduced me to many artworks, which I sketched and filed away to "do something with" someday. I've used many of these as inspiration for the hand knit designs that fill *History on Two Needles*.

### THE JOURNEY

Aside from creating the designs and knitting the garments, patterning, charting, editing, and publishing has proven harder than with any other book I've written.

The different hurdles of this journey – image licensing, historical research, intense redesigning – have made for a long road. But one I have thoroughly enjoyed.

I feel very lucky to have had the chance to create this collection.

## SIZE-ISM & REALISM

I've tried to include a wide range of sizes for all the garments, although in some cases the stitches in a repeat determined how many sizes the pattern could accommodate. *Being a larger woman myself, I feel a traitor to 'my people' if I don't create a few pieces in sizes that would work well for everyone.*

It's unrealistic to think that *every* garment will look good on *every* body, but it's surprising how flattering something can be when it's well fit and worn with confidence.

I used models of various sizes, ages, and shapes – I hope my readers will appreciate the diversity!

## BIAS

I've traveled more extensively in the UK and Ireland than in other countries – the only language in which I'm fluent is English. This has led to a strong British bias in my choice of original artwork to use as inspiration, which is especially noticable in the Renaissance section *(a reflection of my own personal love of the Tudor period of history).*

I tried not to be too wordy when discussing events surrounding the original artwork. This is, after all, a knitting book and not a history book!

## DARK ROOM MAGIC

The models and backgrounds were shot separately and married together with the aid of Photoshop. (I admit this freely, I am not trying to hide anything.) The lighting and poses were chosen to match background images which I had shot on previous trips to Europe, with one exception; the Egyptian background was acquired through a photo bank.

As much as I would have loved to have taken my models with me on photo shoot, it just wasn't in my budget! Perhaps one day I'll be able to afford a round-the-world trip with a full complement of stylists and models for another book. Until that time I have my own travel pictures, the extraordinary portrait photography of Jen Simonson, and my wonderful Minnesota Models! *(Thank you, Ellis, Hannah, Lisa, Debra, Lisa, Kristen, and London for your wonderful modeling!)*

Caryatid from the Erechtheion (detail)
Greece (displayed at the British Museum)
c. 421 B.C.E.

Snake Goddess (detail)
from the Palace of Knossos, Crete.
c. 1600 B.C.E.

# Ancient

## 1981 bce — 421 bce

Offering Bearer Statue,
c. 1981 B.C.E.

Meketre Skirt & Top

Knossos Shrug

Minoan Surplice

Chiton

Whether due to a pre Christian-era attitude of body-aware freedom, breakthroughs in spinning and weaving technologies, or an intuitive sense of proportion and form, ancient garments are surprisingly sophisticated. Modern designers often turn to ancient silhouettes when seeking a simple, elegant line.

The three inspirations in this section are full-body statues; two in miniature and one life-size, which represent idealized beauty around the Mediterreanean Sea, c. 1981-421 bce.

None of the women represented by these pieces are weak; the freedom of movement their garments provide is notable.

**Body-conscious silhouettes were favored by sylph-thin ancient Egyptians. Hand-knit fabric adds an ease of wear to the Meketre Skirt & Top.**

*Background: Egyptian carving on column in Philae temple*

*Garment modeled by Ellis Norris, knit by Annie Modesitt*

# Meketre Skirt & Top

The tiny, stunning figurine discovered in a tomb in Thebes is timeless and jarringly modern in its style, stride, and poise.

Ancient Egyptians were not shy. They appreciated a figure hugging garment (and often wore little at all).

The garment represented on our tiny figurine is believed to have been a beaded net dress, formed of strands of linen and thousands of tiny beads.

Worn over a linen shift, or over bare skin, the net dress would conform to the curves of the wearer's body in a very revealing, body-skimming manner.

To recreate the visual impact of this ancient garment, I utilized an unusual stitch that designer Donna Druchunas calls a "Dipstitch" — a stitch that dips down several rows to create a spike and draw up the fabric.

Although I've used five colors in my dress, a similar effect could be achieved using as few as two colors.

Knit in a more narrow palette, the vertical lines of the set would be emphasized.

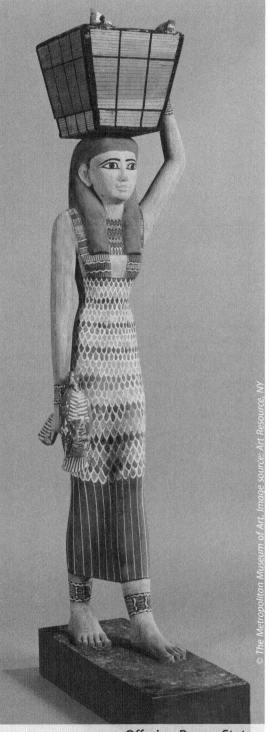

**Offering Bearer Statue,
c. 1981 B.C.E**

## Meketre Skirt & Top Info

| | |
|---|---|
| To Fit Hip/Bust | 28 (34, 40, 46, 52, 58)"/ 71.5 (86.5, 102, 117.5, 132.5, 148) cm |
| Finished Hip | 31 (37, 43, 49, 55, 61)"/ 79 (94, 109.5, 125, 140.5, 155.5) cm, |
| Skirt Length | 34 (35¼, 36½, 37¾, 39, 40¼)"/86.5 (90, 93, 96, 99.5, 102.5) cm |
| Finished Bust | 31 (37, 43, 49, 55, 61)"/ 79 (94.5, 109.5, 125, 140.5, 155.5) cm |
| Top Length | 22¾ (23¾, 24¼, 24¾, 25½, 26)"/ 58 (60.5, 62, 63, 65, 66) cm |
| Skill Level | K 3 Intermediate |
| Fiber | Elsebeth Lavold, Bamboucle (87yds/79m 1.75oz/50gr) Color A #9 Peacock Blue 5 (6, 7, 8, 9, 10) Balls Color B #11 Bright Moss 2 (2, 3, 3, 4, 4) Balls Color C #13 Burnt Orange 3 (4, 4, 5, 6, 6) Balls Color D #4 Sand 4 (5, 6, 6, 7, 7) Balls Color E #10 Moss 5 (6, 7, 8, 9, 10) Balls |
| Gauge | 18 sts x 24 rows = 4"/10cm over charted skirt pattern using size: 8 US/5mm |
| Needle | Size 8 US/5mm 36"/92cm Circular (add'l size: 7US/4.5mm needle) |
| Notions | Stitch marker, darning needle, 1-⅝" elastic (cut to waist measurement + 2"), sewing needle and thread. |

## Meketre Skirt & Top Stitches

St st – Stockinette Stitch
Rev St st — Reverse St st
Sl st wyws – Slip st with yarn to the wrong side
Sl st wyrs – Slip st with yarn to the right side
VDD – Vertical Double Decrease
VDI – Vertical Double Increase
K2tog-R – Knit 2 tog with a right slant
K2tog-L – Knit 2 tog with a left slant
Dipstitch

## Meketre Skirt & Top Techniques

DKSS Edge – Double Knit Slip Stitch Edge

*See Special Techniques, page 116, for full explanations on how to work the stitches and techniques listed above.*

## Dipstitch Texture Pattern

Round 1: [P3, k1, p4, k1, p1] around.
Round 2: With CC [k3, VDD, k3, VDI] around.
Round 3: Knit all sts.
Rep Rounds 2 & 3, twice more, 6 rows in CC total.
Round 8: [K8, DS Knit this loop & next st tog. K1] around.
Round 9: [P3, k1, p4, k1, p1] around.
Round 10: With next CC [k3, VDI, k3, VDD] around.
Round 11: Knit all sts.
Rep Rounds 10 & 11 twice more, 6 rows in CC total.
Round 16: [K3, DS, Knit this loop & next st tog. K1] around.

## Yoke Pattern

Round 1: With C, [k8, k2tog-R] 12 (15, 18, 21, 23, 25) times around.
Round 2: Purl all sts.
Round 3: With D, [k7, k2tog-R], around.
Round 4: Purl all sts.
Rounds 5 & 13: With B, knit all sts.
Rounds 6 & 10: With D [sl 1, k1] around.
Rounds 7 & 11: With A, knit all sts.
Round 9: With C, knit all sts.
Round 14: With D [k6, k2tog-R] around.
Rounds 15 & 19: With D, purl.
Round 16: With B, knit.
Round 17: With B, purl.
Round 18: With D [k5, k2tog-R] around.
Rounds 20 — 28: Rep Rounds 5-13.
Round 29: With D [k4, k2tog-R] around.
Round 30: With D, purl.

**Yoke Slip Stitch Colorwork Detail**

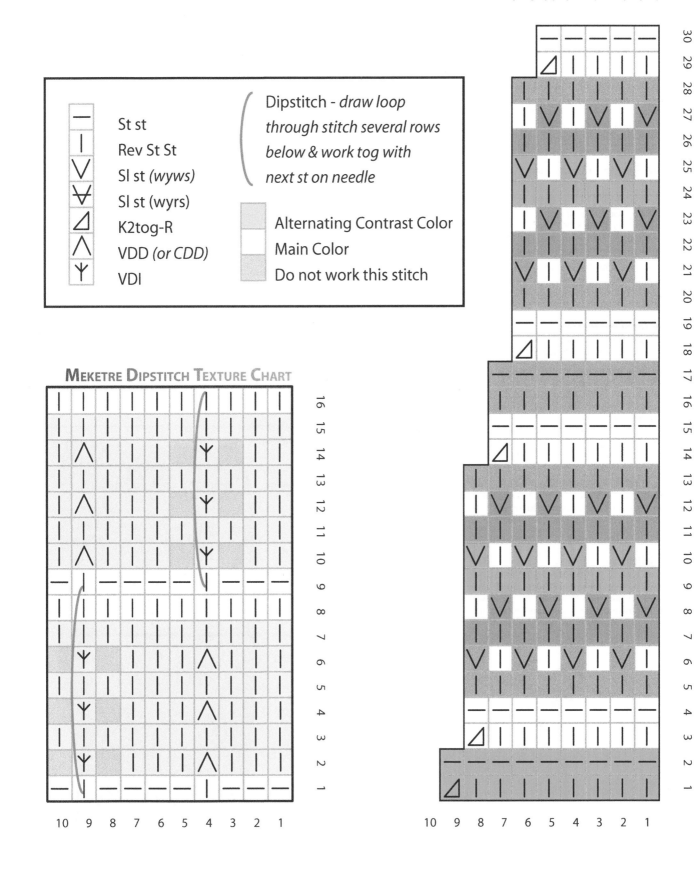

MEKETRE YOKE COLORWORK CHART

Legend:
- — St st
- | Rev St St
- V Sl st (wyws)
- ⩒ Sl st (wyrs)
- ◿ K2tog-R
- ∧ VDD (or CDD)
- Ψ VDI

Dipstitch - *draw loop through stitch several rows below & work tog with next st on needle*

Alternating Contrast Color
Main Color
Do not work this stitch

MEKETRE DIPSTITCH TEXTURE CHART

# MEKETRE SKIRT

### HEM

With larger needles and A, cast on 123 (153, 173, 203, 223, 243) sts. Switch to smaller needles and est ribbing as foll:

Row 1 (RS): K1, sl 1 wyrs, k1 (DKSS edge), [p2, k3] rep to last 5 sts, p2, k1, sl 1 wyrs, k1, (DKSS edge).
Row 2 (WS): Sl 1 wyws, k1, Sl 1 wyws, work in rib as est to last 3 sts, Sl 1 wyws, k1, Sl 1 wyws]. Rep last 2 rows, working first and last 3 sts of each row in double knit slip stitch (DKSS) edging, until piece meas 12 (12½, 13, 13½, 14, 14 ½)"/30.5 (32, 33, 34.5, 35.5, 37) cm from cast on row.

### JOINING THE SKIRT / COLORWORK

Slip sts to larger circ. You will be joining to work in the round at this point.

Bring the tips of the needle together, and re-orient the sts so that the 3 DKSS edge sts alternate with each other (see diagram). From this point the piece will be worked entirely in the round.

Next Round: With D and starting at the point where the DKSS edge sts were merged, place marker to note start of round, [k2tog-L] three times. knit to the end of the round

### ESTABLISH STITCH PATTERN

Note that the start of round marker will move from round to round, readjust as necessary.

Following either written instructions or charted pattern, work Dipstitch Texture Pattern. Use color D as the main color in rounds 1, 8, 9 & 16, and alternate contrasting colors every 8th row, in the following order: C, A, B, E, C, E, until the Dipstitch Texture Pattern section of the skirt meas approx 16 (16½, 17, 17½, 18, 18½)"/41 (42, 43.5, 44.5, 46, 47) cm, ending with Round 1 or 9 of charted pattern.

Change to Color E and work in St st for 6 (6¼, 6½, 6¾, 7, 7¼)"/15.5 (16, 16.5, 17, 18, 18.5) cm. Purl 1 round (turning ridge). Change to smaller circ needles and work in St st for 2"/10cm. Bind of all sts loosely.

## FINISHING

Measure a piece of 1-⅝"/8cm elastic to the desired waist measurement + 2"/10cm. Stitch elastic together, leaving a 1" overlap. Fit the elastic circle into the top of the waist band, turning the facing at the turning ridge. Sew the bound off edge to the WS of the work.

# MEKETRE TOP

### RIBBING

With larger needles and A, cast on 120 (150, 170, 200, 220, 240) sts. Switch to smaller circ needles, join sts, place marker to note start of round and est ribbing as foll:

Round 1 (RS): [P2, k3] 24 (30, 34, 40, 44, 48) times
Rep Round 1 until piece meas 4 (4¼, 4 ½, 4¾, 5, 5¼)"/10 (11, 11.5, 12, 13, 13.5) cm from cast on, or desired length from waist.

### ESTABLISH STITCH PATTERN

Work Colorwork Pattern, from written or charted instructions as you prefer, , changing contrasting colors every 8th row, repeating the order: C, A, B, E, C, E as necessary, until work meas approx 12 (12¼, 12½, 12¾, 13, 13¼)"/30.5 (31.5, 32, 32.5, 33, 34) cm, or desired length. End with Round 7 or 15 of pattern.

Next Round: With larger circ needles and Color D, knit all sts.

### ARMHOLE SHAPING

Round 1: With D, k30 (40, 50, 70, 80, 90) sts, BO next 30 (30, 30, 30, 30, 30) sts, k 30 (50, 60, 70, 80, 90) sts, BO final 30 (30, 30, 30, 30, 30) sts
Round 2: Purl 30 (40, 50, 70, 80, 90) sts, using the cable cast-on method, CO 30 (30, 40, 40, 40, 40) sts, purl 30 (50, 60, 70, 80, 90) sts, cable CO 30 (30, 40, 40, 40, 40) sts – 120 (150, 190, 220, 240, 260) sts total in yoke.

### ESTABLISH YOKE STITCH PATTERN

Working from chart or written instructions as you prefer, work 29 rows of Yoke pattern.

Repeat rounds 29 & 30 0 (1, 1, 1, 2, 2) more times, working 1 st less between decreases than in prev dec round – 60 (60, 72, 84, 69, 75) sts rem around neck edge.

### STITCH COUNTS IN YOKE ROUNDS

Round 1: 108 (135, 162, 189, 207, 225) sts
Round 3: 96 (120, 144, 168, 184, 200) sts
Round 14: 84 (105, 126, 147, 161, 175) sts
Round 18: 72 (90, 108, 126, 138, 150) sts
Round 29: 60 (75, 90, 105, 115, 125) sts
Work 6 rounds in garter stitch (knit 1 round, purl 1 round), bind off all sts loosely.

### FINISHING

Weave in ends, steam block.

**Reseating skirt edge stitches**

## Meketre Top Schematic

15 (15, 18, 21, 17 1/4, 18 3/4)"/
38.5 (38.5, 46, 53.5, 44, 48) cm

6 3/4 (7 1/4, 7 1/4,
7 1/4, 7 1/2, 7 1/2)"/
17 (18.5, 18.5,
18.5, 19, 19) cm

22 3/4 (23 3/4, 24 1/4, 24 3/4, 25 1/2, 26)"/
58 (60.5, 62, 63, 65, 66.5) cm

12 (12 1/4, 12 1/2, 12 3/4, 13, 13 1/4)"/
30.5 (31.5, 32, 32.5, 33, 34) cm

4 (4 1/4, 4 1/2, 4 3/4, 5, 5 1/4)"/
10 (11, 11.5, 12, 13, 13.5) cm

31 (37, 43, 49, 55, 61)"/
79 (94.5, 109.5, 125, 140.5, 155.5) cm

## Meketre Skirt Schematic

6 (6 1/4, 6 1/2,
6 3/4, 7, 7 1/4)"/
15.5 (16, 16.5,
17, 18, 18.5) cm

16 (16 1/2, 17, 17 1/2, 18, 18 1/2)"/
41 (42, 43.5, 44.5, 46, 47) cm

34 (35 1/4, 36 1/2, 37 3/4, 39, 40 1/4)"/ 86.5 (90, 93, 96.5, 99.5, 102.5) cm

12 (12 1/2, 13, 13 1/2, 14, 14 1/2)"/
30.5 (32, 33, 34.5, 35.5, 37) cm

31 (37, 43, 49, 55, 61)"/
79 (94.5, 109.5, 125, 140.5, 155.5) cm

**Center Back Skirt Slit Detail**

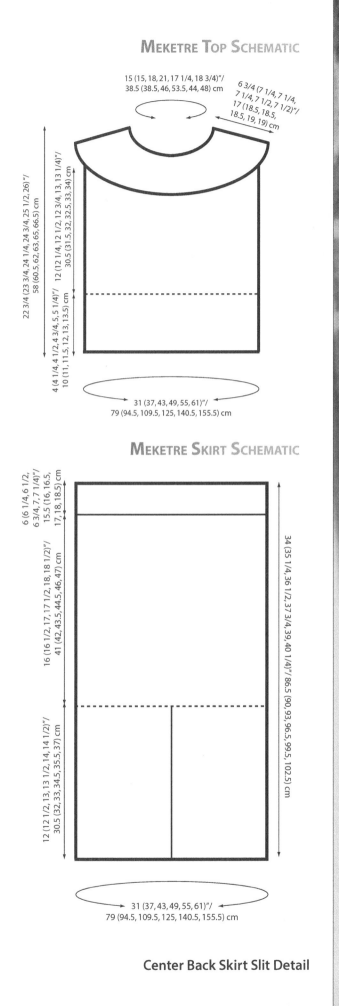

The pattern motifs used in the Knossos Shrug are based on the Snake
Goddess Statue & reflect the strong tradition of Mediterranean weaving.

*Background: Dover Castle Interior*

*Garment modeled by Ellis Norris, knit by Annie Modesitt*

# Knossos Shrug

*Garments from early cultures were generally square or rectangular in shape to utilize every precious woven inch from narrow looms.*

While not generally considered a fashion icon, the Minoan Snake Goddess is known to most of us as a fixture of Art History 101.

A very early example of corsetting (perhaps related to the charmed girdle of Aphrodite), the narrow waist and exaggerated hips and bosom create a strong, iconic female shape.

My own take on the Snake Goddess is a Minoan *Twin Set*: a simple, sleeveless surplice matched with a square-shaped shrug.

The lace pattern used in the shrug is linear, measured, rhythmic, to honor the strong weaving tradition in the Mediterranean.

The pattern of the shrug is very simple: there is no shaping within the garment; instead, the silhouette is achieved by folding and adding a waistband after the main body is finished.

I chose a lovely raw silk by Mango Moon to bridge the simplicity of line with a sophisticated, understated, but luxurious fiber.

*Photo by Chris 73*

**Snake Goddess from the Palace of Knossos, Crete., c. 1600 B.C.E.**

## KNOSSOS SHRUG INFORMATION

| To Fit | 32 (36, 44, 50)"/ 81.5 (92, 112, 127.5) cm bust |
|---|---|
| Finished Bust | 35 (39½, 48½, 55)"/ 89.5 (101, 123.5, 140.5) cm |
| Total Length | 16⅜ (16⅜, 19, 21⅝)"/ 42 (42, 48.5, 55) cm |
| Skill Level | K 3 Intermediate |
| Fiber | Mango Moon, Dharma (150yds/137m) Thyme, 3 (4, 5, 6) skeins |
| Gauge | 12 sts x 16 rows = 4"/10cm in lace pattern using size 9US/5.5mm. |
| Needles | Size 9US/5.5mm needles (add'l size: 8US/6mm) either straight or circular. |
| Notions | Darning needle |

## KNOSSOS SHRUG STITCHES

St st – Stockinette Stitch
Rev St st – Reverse St st
Sl st wyws – Slip st with yarn to the wrong side
Sl st wyrs – Slip st with yarn to the right side
YO – Yarn Over
K2tog-R – Knit 2 tog with a right slant
K2tog-L – Knit 2 tog with a left slant
P2tog-R – Purl 2 tog with a right slant
P2tog-L – Purl 2 tog with a left slant

## KNOSSOS SHRUG TECHNIQUES

DKSS Edge – Double Knit Slip Stitch Edge
3 Needle Bind Off
Cable Cast On
I-Cord Bind Off

*See Special Techniques, page 116, for full explanations on how to work the stitches and techniques listed above.*

## KNOSSOS SHRUG CHART TEXT

Row 1: [P1, YO, p2tog-L, k5] rep to last 3 sts, end p1, YO, p2tog-L
Row 2: K1, YO, k2tog-L, [p5, k1, YO, k2tog-L] rep to end.
Rows 3 & 4: Rep last 2 rows once.
Row 5: [P3, k1, (YO, k2tog-L) twice] rep to last 3 sts, end p3.
Row 6: K3, [P1, (p2tog-L, YO) twice, k3] rep to end.
Rows 7 & 8: Rep last 2 rows once.
Row 9: [P1, YO, p2tog-L, k5] rep to last 3 sts, end p1, YO, p2tog-L
Row 10: K1, YO, k2tog-L, [p5, k1, YO, k2tog-L] rep to end.
Rows 11 & 12: Rep last 2 rows once.
Row 5: [P3, k1, (YO, k2tog-L) twice]

# KNOSSOS SHRUG

## BODY

With smaller needles cast on 70 (70, 86, 102) sts.

Row 1: [K2, p2] rep to last 2 sts, end k2.
Row 2: [P2, k2] rep to last 2 sts, end p2
Cont in k2, p2 ribbing for 2 more rows, dec 3 sts evenly across work in last row — 67 (67, 83, 99) sts.
Change to larger needles and est patt as foll:

## ESTABLISH STITCH PATTERN

Using either Shrug Texture Chart or Shrug Texture Chart Text, rep rows 1-12 until piece meas 17½ (19¾, 24¼, 27½)"/44.5 (50.5, 62, 70) cm, end with row 1, 3, 9 or 11.

Next Row (WS): Loosely bind off 34 (34, 42, 50) sts, cont in patt as est to end of row.
Next Row (RS): Work in patt as est to bound of sts. Using any method, cast on 34 (34, 42, 50) sts.
Next Row (WS): Purl 34 (34, 42, 50) sts, cont in patt as est to end of row.
Next Row (RS): Rep patt as est across entire row,

including new sts at end of row.
Cont working in patt as est until piece meas 35 (39½, 48½, 55)"/89.5 (101, 123.5, 140.5) cm from original cast on row, end with Row 4 of patt, increasing 3 sts evenly across last row of work — 70 (70, 86, 102) sts

Change to smaller needles and work in k2, p2 ribbing for 4 rows. Bind off all sts loosely in rib. Steam block body lightly.

## SHAPING BODY

Fold piece lengthwise and meas 8¾ (9⅞, 12⅛, 13¾)"/22.5 (25, 31, 35) cm in from start of ribbing at either end of piece, pin edges together at this point.

With darning needle and a strand of yarn, stitch along edge from pinned point to ribbed cuff on either end of piece (sleeves) leaving 17½ (19¼, 24¼, 27½)"/44.5 (50.5, 62, 70) cm across the back edge and 8¾ (9⅞, 12⅛, 13¾)"/22.5 (25, 31, 35) cm at either front open.

## BOTTOM RIBBING

With smaller needles and right side of work facing, starting at lower left front edge pick up and knit 106 (122, 146, 166) sts around bottom edge.

Next Row (WS): [P2, k2] rep to end of round, end p2.

Cont in k2, p2 ribbing for 5"/13cm. Bind off all sts loosely in rib.

## NECK OPENING

With smaller needle and right side of work facing, starting at lower right front edge of waist ribbing, PU and knit 92 (92, 108, 124) sts around entire neck edge. With larger needles knit all sts. Work I-Cord bind off across all sts, tie off last st.

## FINISHING

Steam block ribbing and neck edge.

**KNOSSOS SHRUG TEXTURE CHART**

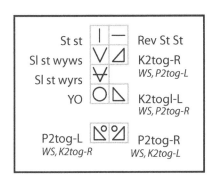

| | | | | |
|---|---|---|---|---|
| St st | ǀ | — | Rev St St | |
| Sl st wyws | V | ◿ | K2tog-R | *WS, P2tog-L* |
| Sl st wyrs | ∀ | | | |
| YO | ◯ | ◹ | K2togl-L | *WS, P2tog-R* |
| P2tog-L | ◹° | °◺ | P2tog-R | |
| *WS, K2tog-R* | | | *WS, K2tog-L* | |

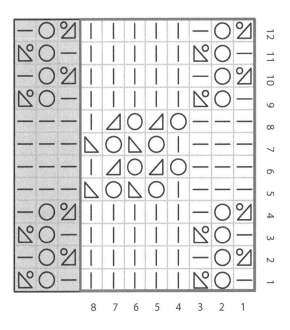

**KNOSSOS SHRUG SCHEMATIC**

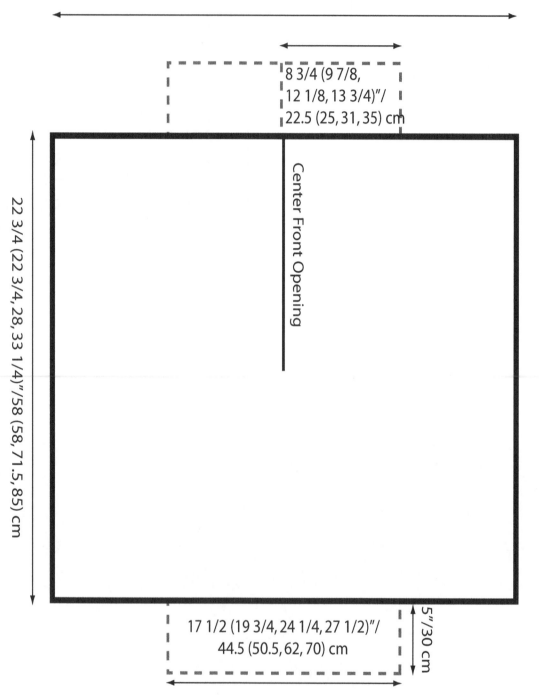

35 (39 1/2, 48 1/2, 55)"/89.5 (101, 123.5, 140.5) cm

8 3/4 (9 7/8, 12 1/8, 13 3/4)"/ 22.5 (25, 31, 35) cm

Center Front Opening

22 3/4 (22 3/4, 28, 33 1/4)"/58 (58, 71.5, 85) cm

17 1/2 (19 3/4, 24 1/4, 27 1/2)"/ 44.5 (50.5, 62, 70) cm

5"/30 cm

**The Minoan Surplice can be worn closed, tied at the waist with a ribbon, or left open over a camisole.**

*Background: Dover Castle Interior*

*Garment modeled by Ellis Norris, knit by Annie Modesitt*

# Minoan Surplice

It is easy to regard the statuette of the Snake Goddess as an example of elegance, gracefulness, and a sense of fashion.

It is difficult to know the exact purpose or meaning behind the tiny figurine known to us as the "Minoan Snake Goddess."

Was she a religious figure? A fertility goddess, as many archaeologists have posited?

Or was she simply a representation of the average wealthy, snake-loving woman of Crete (*Minoan Snake-Handler Barbie*)?

What is not in question is that her clothing is notable, and vividly portrayed in this three-dimensional object. The heavy skirt, perhaps panels of felted wool, hang in stark contrast to the light, bare bodice and decorative girdle.

The tight sleeves, waist, and double apron denote a culture with draping, fitting, and sewing skills.

In my Surplice Top, I've chosen to once again use a stitch pattern that echoes the Minoan weaving tradition, but this time with a bit of shaping added at the fronts to create the easy drape of the cross-over shape.

**Snake Goddess
from the Palace of Knossos, Crete.,
c. 1600 B.C.E.**

## MINOAN SURPLICE INFORMATION

| | |
|---|---|
| To Fit Bust | 32 (35, 38, 41, 44, 48, 52)"/ 82 (90, 97.5, 105, 113, 123, 133) cm |
| Finished Bust | 38 (41, 44, 47, 50, 54, 58)"/97.5 (105, 113, 120.5, 128, 138.5, 148) cm |
| Total Length | 18½ (19½, 21½, 23, 24½, 26½, 28)"/47.4 (50, 55, 59, 63, 68, 72) cm |
| Skill Level | K 3 Intermediate |
| Fiber | Mango Moon, Dharma (150yds/137m) Wheat, 3 (3, 4, 4) skeins |
| Gauge | 12sts x 16 rows = 4"/10cm over texture stitch patt using needle size: 9US/5.5mm. |
| Needle | 9US/5.5mm. |
| Notions | Safety pins (2), 24" ribbons for closure hook & eye for closure (optional), extra needle for 3-needle bind off. |

## MINOAN SURPLICE STITCHES

St st – Stockinette Stitch
Rev St st – Reverse St st
Sl st wyws – Slip st with yarn to the wrong side
Sl st wyrs – Slip st with yarn to the right side
YO – Yarn Over
K2tog-R – Knit 2 tog with a right slant
K2tog-L – Knit 2 tog with a left slant
P2tog-R – Purl 2 tog with a right slant
P2tog-L – Purl 2 tog with a left slant

## MINOAN SURPLICE TECHNIQUES

DKSS Edge – Double Knit Slip Stitch Edge
3 Needle Bind Off
Cable Cast On
I-Cord Bind Off

*See Special Techniques, page 116, for full explanations on how to work the stitches and techniques listed above.*

## MINOAN SURPLICE EYELET RIB

Row 1: K1, sl 1 wyrs, k1 (DKSS edge), p2tog-L, YO, [k2, p2tog-L, YO] rep 28 (30, 32, 34, 37, 40, 43) times to last 5 sts, end p2, DKSS edge.
Row 2: Sl 1 wyws, k1, sl 1 wyws (DKSS edge), (k2tog-L, YO, p2) rep to last 5 sts, end k2, DKSS edge.
Rep last 2 rows 3 more times for a total of 8 rows of eyelet rib.

## MINOAN SURPLICE TRIANGLE

Rows 1 & 9 (RS): (P1, k4, p1) rep to end.
Rows 2 & 8 (WS): (P4, k2) rep to end.
Rows 3 & 7 (RS): (P3, k3) rep to end.
Rows 4 & 6 (WS): (P2, k4) rep to end.
Row 5 (RS): (P5, k1) rep to end.
Rows 10 & 16 (RS): (K2, p4) rep to end.
Rows 11 & 15 (RS): (K3, p3) rep to end.
Rows 12 & 14 (WS): (K4, p2) rep to end.
Row 13 (RS): (K1, p5) rep to end.

# MINOAN SURPLICE

### EYELET RIB

Cast on 124 (132, 140, 148, 160, 172, 184) sts, est rib as foll (follow charted pattern if desired.)

Row 1: K1, sl 1 wyrs, k1 (DKSS edge), p2tog-L, YO, [k2, p2tog-L, YO] rep 28 (30, 32, 34, 37, 40, 43) times to last 5 sts, end p2, k1, sl 1 wyrs, k1
Row 2: Sl 1 wyws, k1, sl 1 wyws, (k2tog-L, YO, p2) rep to last 5 sts, end k2, sl 1 wyws, k1, sl 1 wyws.
Rep last 2 rows 3 more times for a total of 8 rows of eyelet rib.
Next row (RS): Knit all sts, inc 0 (4, 2, 6, 0, 0, 0) sts evenly across row — 124 (136, 142, 154, 160, 172, 184) sts

### EST TRIANGLE PATTERN

Next row (RS): K1, sl 1 wyrs, k1, p2, rep sts 1-6 of row 1 of chart 19 (21, 22, 24, 25, 27, 29) times to last 5 sts, end p2, k1, sl 1 wyrs, k1.
Next row (WS): Sl 1 wyws, k1, sl 1 wyws, k2, work in charted pat as est to last 5 sts, end k2, sl 1 wyws, k1, sl 1 wyws.

Cont working 5 edge sts on either side in Double Knit Slip Stitch edging + 2 rev st st gutter sts (as est in ribbing, in grey in chart), while working sts in between edges in charted patt as est.

Work until piece meas 8 (8½, 9½, 10½, 11½, 12½, 13½)"/20.5 (21.5, 24, 27, 29.5, 32, 34.5) cm from cast on. End with a WS row. Mark the last st on either end of this row with a safety pin.

### NECK SHAPING

Begin shaping neck / body as foll:

Next row (RS): Work 17 sts in patts as est, k2tog-L, P2 (2, 1, 1, 2, 2, 2) sts, [k2, p2] rep until 19 sts rem (ending purl 2 (2, 1, 1, 2, 2, 2) sts), k2tog-R, work in patts as est to end of row.
Next row (WS): Cont in patt as est, work 17 sts, p2tog-L, work in rib as est in prev row until 19 sts rem, p2tog-R, work rem sts in patt as est.
Work last 2 rows a total of 6 (7, 7, 8, 8, 9, 9) times until 100 (108, 114, 122, 128, 136, 148) sts rem total.
Work even with no further decreasing until piece meas 11 (11½, 12½, 13½, 14½, 15½, 16½)"/28 (29.5, 32, 34.5, 37, 39.5, 42) cm from CO. End with a WS row.

### DIVIDE FRONTS FROM BACK

Next Row (RS): Work 26 (28, 28, 32, 30, 32, 34) sts in patt as est, slip these onto a holder to work later (Right Front). Work 48 (52, 56, 60, 68, 72, 80) sts in patt as est (Back).
Slip rem 26 (28, 28, 32, 30, 32, 34) sts onto holder to work later (Left Front).

### BACK

Work Back sts only in ribbing as est with no decreasing, working first and last 3 sts of each row in DKSS edge as with front edges as foll:

Next Row (RS): K1, sl 1 wyrs, k1, work in rib as est to last 3 sts, k1, sl 1 wyrs, k1.
Next row (WS): Sl 1 wyws, k1, sl 1 wyws, work in rib as est to last 3 sts, sl 1 wyws, k1, sl 1 wyws.
Cont with no decreasing until Back meas 7½ (8, 9, 9½, 10, 11, 11½)"/19 (20.5, 23, 24, 25.5, 28, 29.5) cm from Fronts/Back division. Do not bind off, set sts aside to work later.

## Detail of the Triangle Texture Pattern

## FRONTS

Slip Left Front sts onto needle and work one WS row in patt as est. Turn. Working both Fronts together:

Next Row (Left Front RS): Work in patts as est to last 3 sts of Left Front, k1, sl 1 wyrs, k1. Work Right Front as for Left.
Next Row (Right Front WS): Work in patts as est to last 3 sts, sl 1 wyws, k1, sl 1 wyws. Work Left Front as for Right.
Rep last 2 rows until Fronts meas same as Back.

### SHOULDER JOIN

Arrange Left Front sts and Back sts on two needles so that the Right Sides of work are facing each other. With the WS of the Left Front toward you, and starting at the armhole edge, join the first 16 (18, 18, 22, 20, 22, 24) sts of the Left Front & Back using a 3 needle bind off, cut yarn, leaving a 8"/20cm tail.

Repeat the 3-needle bind off with the Right Front on the opposite edge of the Back. 10 sts rem unworked for each Front, 16 (16, 20, 16, 28, 28, 32) sts rem unworked at the center Back.

### BACK NECK SHAPING

Slip 10 sts from Right Front, 16 (16, 20, 16, 28, 28, 32) center back neck sts, then 10 sts from Left Front onto the same needle — 36 (36, 40, 36, 48, 48, 52) sts

The Left Front sts should be closest to the tip and ready to be worked, the WS should be facing you.

Next row (WS): Sl 1 wyws, k1, sl 1 wyws, k2, [p1, k1] 2 times, p1, k2tog-L, W&T.
Next row (RS): [k1, p1] 3 times, p2, k1, sl 1 wyrs, k1. Rep last 2 rows until 21 sts rem (10 unworked from Right Front and 11 which have become the Back collar) to be worked.

### JOIN RIGHT SHOULDER

Arrange sts, 10 on one needle & 11 on another, so the neck edge sts are farthest away from the needle points.

With right sides together and wrong sides facing, join sts using a 3-needle bind off.

### FINISHING

Weave in ends and steam block.

Try on vest and, at row where safety pins are at edges, attach a closure to allow the vest to cross itself and close. In the sample a ribbon was attached to the Left Front edge, and a corresponding ribbon was attached to the right side of the Right Front approx 3"/7.5 cm from the edge. A second closure like a snap or hook and eye can be attached to the Right Front edge and wrong side of Left Front for a more secure fit.

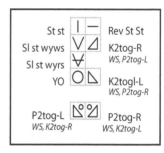

| | | | |
|---|---|---|---|
| St st | I — | Rev St St | |
| Sl st wyws | V ◿ | K2tog-R WS, P2tog-L | |
| Sl st wyrs | ⩜ | | |
| YO | O ◺ | K2togl-L WS, P2tog-R | |
| P2tog-L WS, K2tog-R | ◹ ◸ | P2tog-R WS, K2tog-L | |

## MINOAN SURPLICE TRIANGLE CHART

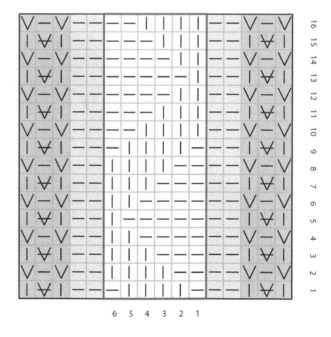

## MINOAN SURPLICE EYELET RIB

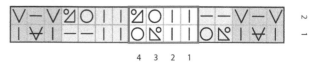

## MINOAN SURPLICE SCHEMATIC

8 3/4 (9 1/4, 9 1/4, 10 3/4, 10, 10 3/4, 11 1/4)"/ 22.5 (23.5, 23.5, 27.5, 25.5, 27.5, 28.5) cm

16 (17 1/4, 18 3/4, 20, 22 3/4, 24, 26 3/4)"/ 41 (44, 48, 51, 58, 61, 68) cm

7 1/2 (8, 8 1/2, 8 1/2, 9, 9, 9 1/2)"/ 19 (20.5, 21.5, 21.5, 23, 23, 24) cm

11 (11 1/2, 11 1/2, 12, 12, 12 1/2, 12 1/2)"/ 28 (29.5, 29.5, 30.5, 30.5, 32, 32) cm

38 (41, 44, 47, 50, 54, 58)"/97 (104.5, 112, 120, 127.5, 138, 148) cm

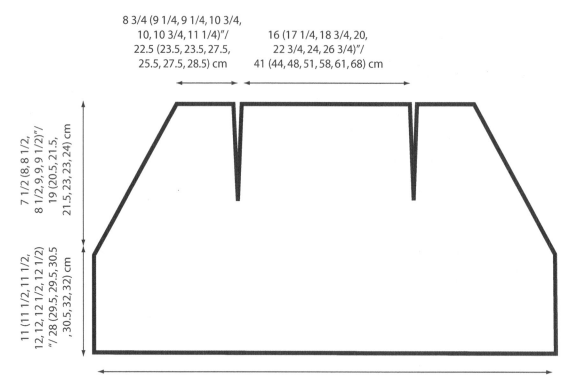

I call the pleats of the Chiton *'faux fortuny pleating'*, created by slipping a stitch in the center of an odd number of rib stitches.
*Background: Column in Rome*
*Chiton modeled by Lisa Genis, Garment hand knit by Miriam Tegels*

# Chiton

*The simplicity of Greek clothing is proof that the most important element in fashion is the human body.*

The *Chiton* was the T-shirt of ancient Greece. It was worn by all classes, the length of the chiton being one of the main determiners of the wearer's status.

Women and older upper-class men wore longer chitons, while male workers and soldiers generally wore the shortest chitons.

When the chiton traveled to Rome it became known as the *tunica*, but it continued to cross classes as the most mobile of garments.

What differentiated the chiton was the fit. It was loose *(often cut longer than the wearer's height)* with the excess fabric belted at the natural waist by a *zoster*, or girdle.

By not requiring constant readjustment of large amounts of fabric, a chiton was freeing. Its beauty came from a sense of simplicity and fine fabric, often made of linen or wool, which draped beautifully.

My own chiton is knit of a blend of bison, cashmere, silk, and tencel from Buffalo Gold, which *also* drapes beautifully!

*Photo Raminus Falcon*

**The Charioteer of Delphi, bronze, Delphi Museum, Greece c. 470 B.C.E.**

## CHITON INFORMATION

| To Fit Bust | 32 (36, 40, 44, 48, 52)"/81.5 (92, 102, 112, 122.5, 132.5)cm |
|---|---|
| Fin Bust | 47½ (51, 56½, 61½, 65, 70½)"/121 (130, 144, 157, 166, 180)cm |
| Length | 30 (33, 36, 39, 42, 45, 50)"/ 76.5 (84, 92, 99.5, 107, 115)cm |
| Skill Level | K3 Intermediate, some crochet. |
| Fiber | Buffalo Gold Lux #12 (300yds/274m 1.4oz/40gr) Natural, 2 (3, 4, 5, 6, 7) skeins |
| Gauge | 28 sts x 24 rows = 4"/10cm over rib pattern at rest, with no stretch, using size 6US/4mm needles. |
| Needles | Size 6US/4mm needles. |
| Notions: | Approx 600-1100 6/0 green tone glass beads (chiton), 250 gold tone glass beads (belt and finishing), darning needle, waste yarn, size US G-6/4mm crochet hook for joining and belt. |

## CHITON STITCHES

St st – Stockinette Stitch
Rev St st — Reverse St st
Sl st wyws – Slip st with yarn to the wrong side
Sl st wyrs – Slip st with yarn to the right side
SB – Slide Bead
Ch 1 – Chain 1
Sc – Single Crochet
Dc – Double Crochet
Bch – Beaded Chain
BSc – Beaded Single Crochet

## CHITON TECHNIQUES

I-Cord used to make belt ties.
DKSS Edge – Double Knit Slip Stitch Edge

*See Special Techniques, page 116, for full explanations on how to work the stitches and techniques listed above.*

## CHITON GARTER BEADED EDGE

Rows 1 & 3 (RS): [K1, sl 1 wyrs, k1] (DKSS edge), p2, k to last 5 sts, p2, DKSS edge.
Row 2 (WS): Sl 1 wyws, k1, sl 1 wyws, (DKSS edge), p2, [(k2, sl b) twice, k1, sl b] rep to last 5 sts, p2, DKSS edge.
Row 4 (WS): Sl 1 wyws, k1, sl 1 wyws, p2, [k1, sl b, (k2, sl b) twice] rep to last 5 sts, p2, DKSS edge.
Rep 4 rows, cont DKSS edges as est.

## CHITON SLIP STITCH RIB

Row 1 (RS): [K1, sl 1 wyrs, k1] (DKSS edge), [k1, sl 1, k1, p3] until 6 sts rem, k1, sl 1, k1, DKSS edge.
Row 2 (WS): [Sl 1 wyws, k1, sl 1 wyws], (DKSS edge), [k3, p3] until 6 sts rem, p3, DKSS edge.
Rep 2 rows, cont DKSS edges as est.

## CHITON

### BEFORE YOU START
*String 296 (344, 384, 432, 480, 520) green beads each onto 2 balls of yarn, set 1 aside for Back (total 592 (688, 768, 864, 960, 1040) beads 6/0 green tone glass beads).*

### FRONT & BACK
*Worked from the neck edge to the hem.*

With a strand of yarn CO 195 (225, 250, 280, 310, 335) sts. Working from written or charted instructions as you prefer, work 4 rows total of Beaded Garter Edge, then work 8 more rows with no beading, 12 rows total. Inc 4 (Dec 2, Inc 3, Inc 3, Dec 3, Inc 2) sts across last WS row — 199 (223, 253, 283, 307, 337) sts

### EST RIB PAT
Working from written or charted instructions as you prefer, work in Slip Stitch Rib Patt (continue working DKSS edges) until piece meas 10 (11, 12, 13, 14, 15)"/25.5 (28, 30.5, 33, 35.5, 38.5)cm from cast on. End with a WS row.

### SHAPE SLEEVES
Next 2 rows: BO 28 (35, 42, 49, 56, 63) sts, work in patt as est to end of row–143 (153, 169, 185, 195, 211) sts rem to be worked as body of piece.

Cont working in patt as est until piece meas 20 (22, 24, 26, 28, 30)"/51 (56, 61, 66.5, 71.5, 76.5)cm from sleeve bind off. Work 8 rows of garter with no beads, then work 4 rows of beaded garter as at start (omitting DKSS edge). BO all sts loosely.

Repeat above for Back.

### FINISHING
Steam block pieces, taking care to stretch the ribbing only slightly. Fold piece vertically at the center and with a piece of waste yarn mark each side of neck opening from center point 5 (5¼, 5½, 5¾, 5 ¾, 5¾)"/13 (13.5, 14, 14.5, 14.5, 14.5)cm from center fold. (Total neck opening 10 (10½, 11, 11½, 11½, 11 ½)"/25.5 (27, 28, 29.5, 29.5, 29.5)cm). Sew underarm and side seams using any stitching method. Join the shoulders as follow:

### SHOULDER SEAM
String approx 50 gold beads onto one ball of yarn. With the crochet hook join yarn to right sleeve end of front, bsc, ch 3, join yarn to right sleeve end of back with a bsc. From this point you'll be working back and forth between the Front and Back along the shoulder as foll:

[Ch 3, sk 2 sts from last join point on Front, bsc on Front, ch 3, sk 2 sts from last join point on Back, bsc on Back] rep to waste yarn marking start of neck opening, tie off yarn after final bsc. Turn work and repeat at opposite (left) side. Weave in ends.

**Shoulder seam and belt crocheted detail**

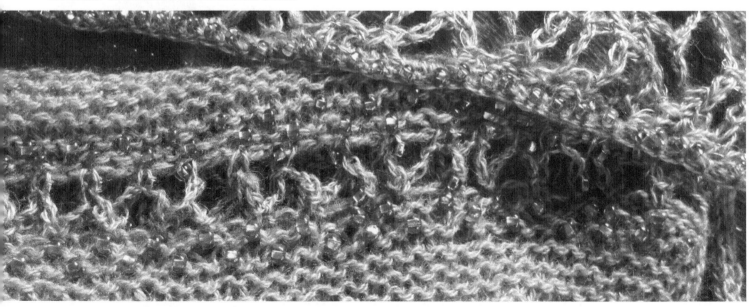

## CHITON TRINITY LACE (CROCHET)

*Multiple of 8 + 9*

To Start: Chain a multiple of 8 + 9.

Row 1: Working 1 ch from hook, sc 1 into each next 3 ch, [ch 5, sk 3 ch, sc 1 into each next 5 ch] rep until 3 ch rem, sc 1 into each next 3 ch. Turn work.

Row 2: Ch 1, sc 1 into each next 2 sc, [sk 1 sc, ch 3, sc 1 into 5-ch sp, ch 3, sk 1 sc, sc 1 into each next 3 sc] rep until 3 sc rem, sc 1 into last 5-ch sp, ch 3, sk 1 sc, sc 1 into each next 2 sc. Turn work.

Row 3: Ch 1, 1 sc, [sk 1 sc, ch 3, 1 sc into 3-ch sp, 1 sc, 1 sc into 3-ch sp, ch 3, sk 1 sc, 1 sc] rep to end, turn work.

Row 4: Ch 5 (counts as turning ch and ch-3), [1 sc into 3-ch sp, sc 1 into each next 3 sc, 1 sc into 3-ch sp, ch 5, sk 1 sc] rep until 2 3-ch sps rem, 1 sc into 3-ch sp, sc 1 into each next 3 sc, 1 sc into 3-ch sp, ch 2, dc into last sc, turn work.

Row 5: Ch 1, 1 sc into dc, [ch 3, sk 1 sc, 1 sc into each next 3 sc, sk 1 sc, ch 3, 1 sc into 5-ch sp] rep to end, turn work.

Row 6: Ch 1, [1 sc, 1 sc into 3-ch sp, ch 3, sk 1 sc, 1 sc, sk 1 sc, ch 3, 1 sc into 3-ch sp] rep to last sc, end 1 sc, turn work.

### BELT (GIRDLE)

The belt shown on the garment was crocheted using the charted trinity lace pattern. You can choose to make your belt any length, from body skimming to long enough to wrap around your waist several times. Work up a swatch using the trinity lace pattern to determine how many total stitches you would like in your belt, a swatch is VERY helpful in this step!

Create a beaded chain using the bch technique a multiple of 8 + 9 (see Trinity Lace Chart for clarification). Work 1 bead into each chain st. Following the chart or written instructions for the Trinity Lace, work 6 row repeat 3 times, *(I started by chaining 89 and working 10 repeats of the pattern)* ending by working Row 1 of chart across entire belt, working each sc as a bsc and working 3 sc into each 5-ch sp.

### TAPERED BELT END

Turn work and working across one end, sc 12 across end of belt. [Turn work, sk 1 sc, work to 1 st before last sc.] rep until 2 sts rem, tie off work. Join a crocheted chain or piece of I-cord to the point as a belt closure. Repeat for other end of belt. Weave in ends and steam block belt.

*Note: For a very firm belt, a strand of fine 36-gauge wire can be crocheted along with the yarn when creating the trinity lace. Experiment with this technique in a swatch to see if it gives you the firm fabric you would like.*

## Caryatid from the Erechtheion (displayed at the British Museum), c. 421 B.C.E.

*Photo Marie-Lan Nguyen*

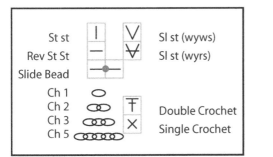

| | | | |
|---|---|---|---|
| St st | | | Sl st (wyws) |
| Rev St St | | | Sl st (wyrs) |
| Slide Bead | | | |
| Ch 1 | | | |
| Ch 2 | | Double Crochet | |
| Ch 3 | | Single Crochet | |
| Ch 5 | | | |

## CHITON SLIP STITCH RIB (WITH DKSS EDGES)

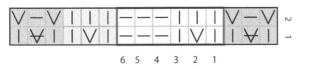

6 5 4 3 2 1

## CHITON BEADED GARTER (WITH DKSS EDGES)

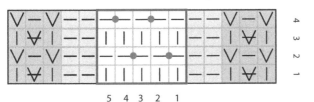

5 4 3 2 1

## CHITON BELT TRINITY LACE (CROCHET)

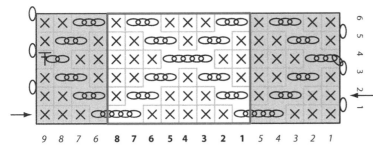

9 8 7 6   8 7 6 5 4 3 2 1   5 4 3 2 1

## CHITON SCHEMATIC

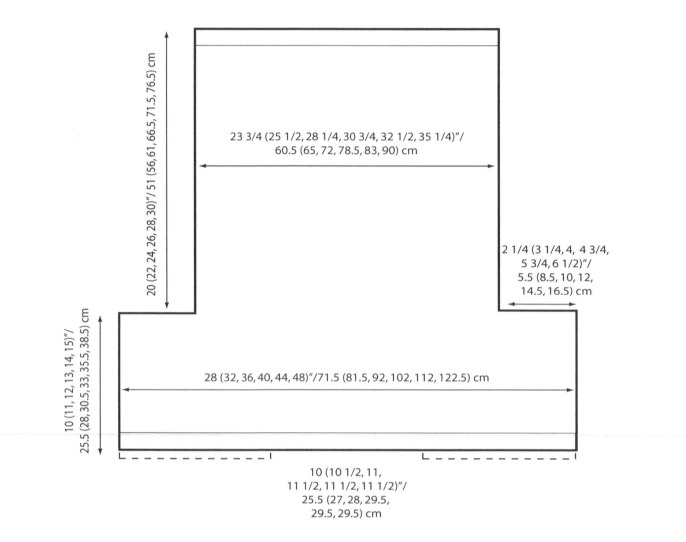

23 3/4 (25 1/2, 28 1/4, 30 3/4, 32 1/2, 35 1/4)"/
60.5 (65, 72, 78.5, 83, 90) cm

20 (22, 24, 26, 28, 30)"/ 51 (56, 61, 66.5, 71.5, 76.5) cm

2 1/4 (3 1/4, 4, 4 3/4,
5 3/4, 6 1/2)"/
5.5 (8.5, 10, 12,
14.5, 16.5) cm

10 (11, 12, 13, 14, 15)"/
25.5 (28, 30.5, 33, 35.5, 38.5) cm

28 (32, 36, 40, 44, 48)"/71.5 (81.5, 92, 102, 112, 122.5) cm

10 (10 1/2, 11,
11 1/2, 11 1/2, 11 1/2)"/
25.5 (27, 28, 29.5,
29.5, 29.5) cm

**Buffalo Wool *LUX* yarn and beads used for the Chiton**

Chiton Shoulder Seam

Caryatids on the
south porch of the Erechtheion,
c. 421 B.C.E.

Photo Dennis Jarvis

Sutton Hoo Helmet
(displayed at the
British Museum),
c. 600

Edward of Woodstock,
The Black Prince
Canterbury Cathedral
c. 1376

# Medieval
## 600 – 1443

Believed to be
Lady Margaret Beaufort
c. 1443

Sutton Hoo Helm

Lady Margaret Scarf

Woodville Tunic

Black Prince Hood

After brilliant strides in fashion in early history, clothing technology seemed to stagnate in the early medieval period, gathering steam once again in late medieval years.

Shapes were simple, allowing fabric and metallic detail to shine through.

The pieces in this section highlight the use of strategically placed detail to augment basic rectangular shapes.

Jacquard stitching, chain embroidery, and cable embellishment are used to create texture and depth, echoing the metallic and fabric embellishments of the period.

Fine goldwork twists from the original Sutton Hoo Helm are recreated in the knitted mask using six-stitch braided cables.

*Background: Newgrange, County Meath, Ireland*

*Sutton Hoo Helm modeled by Lisa Pannell, knit by Annie Modesitt*

Garment & Background Photos Annie Modesitt

# Sutton Hoo Helm

A terrifying visage was half the battle in 7th C. Saxon England, Reconstructed in wool, it is still pretty frightening.

In 1938, an excavation was begun in Sutton Hoo, Suffolk, England, which unearthed one of the most stunning and complete archeological finds in England.

The discovery awakened a new interest in the early medieval period, and shed light on what had previously been considered a 'dark age' in history.

The site, a large burial ship, is almost certainly the grave of a great warrior, perhaps of Rædwald, the ruler of the East Angles.

*Photo Marie-Lan Nguyen*

**Sutton Hoo Helmet
(displayed at the British Museum)
c. 600**

*Gernot Keller*

A first reconstruction in the 1940's, based on preconcieved notions of the Saxon period, was discarded in 1968 and a new reconstruction in the early 21st century *(at left)* was based more firmly on the evidence of the fragments themselves.

My own knitted fabric take on the Sutton Hoo Helm is a simplified version of the original. It is a challenging knit, not to be taken on lightly!

## SUTTON HOO HELM INFORMATION

| To fit head | 19¼ (20¼, 21¾, 23)"/ 49 (51.5, 55.5, 58.5) cm |
|---|---|
| Neck Length | 7 (7½, 8, 8½)"/ 18 (19, 20.5, 21.5) cm |
| Head Length | 9¾ (10¼, 11, 11½)"/ 25 (26, 28, 29.5) cm |
| Fin Head Circ | 20¼ (21¼, 22¾, 24)"/ 51.5 (54, 58, 61) cm |
| Skill Level | K 4 Advanced |
| Fiber | Hazel Knits, Artisan Sock (400yds/365m 4.2oz/120gr) Color A (Neck Color) Woodland, 1 ball all sizes Color B (Face & Head) Hoppy Blonde, 1 ball all sizes |
| Gauge | 26 sts x 38 rows = 4"/10cm worked in St st (flat) using size 3US/3.25mm. |
| Needle: size | Size 3US/3.25mm 24" circular, dpns for tip of helmet (optional) |
| Notions | Darning needle, cable needle, stitch markers |

## SUTTON HOO HELM STITCHES

St st – Stockinette Stitch
Rev St st — Reverse St st
GR Inc – Grandma Right Increase
GL Inc – Grandma Left Increase
W&T – Wrap & Turn
K2tog-R – Knit 2 tog with a right slant
K2tog-L – Knit 2 tog with a left slant
VDD – Vertical Double Decrease
Sl st wyws – Slip st with yarn to the wrong side

## SUTTON HOO HELM TECHNIQUES

Cable Cast On
C4R – Cable 4 Right
C4L – Cable 4 Left
Braid Right
Braid Left

*See Special Techniques, page 116, for full explanations on how to work the stitches and techniques listed above.*

## CHART 1 LOWER CHIN

Rounds 1 & 2: Work in rib as est.
Row 3: (RS): Work in rib as est to 1 st past CF marker W&T.
Row 4 (WS): Work in rib as est to 1 st past CF marker, W&T.
Row 5: Work in rib as est to previously wrapped st, slip wraps onto needle and work tog with wrapped st, work 1 st in rib as est, W&T.
Rounds 6-18: Rep Row 5 until there are 15 sts between W&T & center marker, end with a WS row.
Round 19 (RS): Work to end of round in ribbing as set, working wrapped st together with its wrap.
Rounds 20 & 21: Work 2 rounds in rib as est.
Round 22: Purl 1 round.

# SUTTON HOO HELM

## NECK

With Yarn A, CO 120 (128, 136, 144) sts. Place marker to note start of round, join work.

Work in St st until work meas 4"/10cm.

Next Round: K1, [p2, k2] until 23 (27, 31, 35) sts are worked, place Left side (LS) marker (wide blue line on the charts). Cont in rib across next 37 (37, 37, 37), place Center Front (CF) marker (purple on the chart), cont in rib across next 37 (37, 37, 37) sts place Right side (RS) marker (narrow blue line on the charts), cont to end across last 23 (27, 31, 35) sts of round.

Work in rib as est for 8 rounds.

[Purl 1 round, knit 1 round] twice, then purl 1 more round (5 rounds of garter stitch total)

Rep last 13 rounds (rib and garter) until neck length meas approx 7 (7½, 8, 8½)"/18 (19, 20.5, 21.5) cm from cast on, or desired length of full neck depth.

## FACE

The face is worked predominately in short rows across the 74 center front stitches only. At this point you will work back and forth in rows until the crown, working the face in Color B and the sides and back in Color A, adding and changing colors as directed below.

Working from written instructions or following the charts below as you prefer, work as foll:

### CHART 1 LOWER CHIN SHAPING
Rows 1-22

### CHART 2 UPPER CHIN
Rows 1-44

### CHART 3 NOSE TIP
Rows 1-45-50

At this point you will return to working across all stitches, using 3 balls of yarn (2 balls of A and 1 ball

of B), slipping wraps onto needle and working tog with wrapped sts as in previous rows and changing colors at sides of face as est.

*Note: For a longer nose, rep Rounds 47-50 once or twice more.*

### CHART 4 NOSE BRIDGE SHAPING
Rows 51-68

### CHART 5 EYELID SHAPING
Rows 69 & 70

### CHART 6 BROW
Rows 1-8

After finishing Rounds 1-8, Break B.

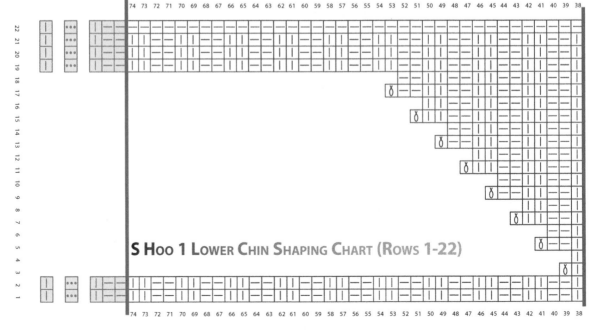

S HOO 1 LOWER CHIN SHAPING CHART (ROWS 1-22)

## CHART 7 CROWN
Rows 1-30

*Note: At this part join sts at the center back, placing marker to note start of round.*

*Be sure to pay attention to the colored lines on the chart. When working the Left side section (before marker), work to the line for your size, and then skip ahead to the 10-st ribbed section; work across center section in full; when working Right side section (after marker), work the 10-st ribbed section, then skip to the line for your size and work to end of round.*

## FINISHING

Divide the rem 20 (22, 22, 22) sts into two groups of sts, a front group and a back group, matching the center front VDD to the center back.

With a darning needle and using the Kitchener stitch (or whatever grafting method you prefer) join the stitches to create a seam across the top of the helm.

With a strand of A and a darning needle, sew up center back seam.

Weave in ends and steam block helmet.

## CHART 2 UPPER CHIN

Row 1: With A, Cont in rib as est, work to left side marker. Join Yarn B, K4, [p3, Braid Left] seven times, p3, k4, W&T.

Row 2: P4, [k3, p6] seven times, k3, p3, W&T (1 st before left side marker.)

Row 3: K3, [p3, Braid Right] seven times, p3, k3, W&T.

Row 4: P3, [k3, p6] four times, k1, W&T.

Row 5: P1, Braid Left, p1, W&T.

Row 6: K1, p6, k2, W&T.

Row 7: P2, Braid Right, p2, W&T.

Row 8 K2, p6, k3, p6, k1, W&T.

Row 9: P1, [Braid Left, p3] twice, Braid Left, p1, W&T.

Row 10: K1, [p6, k3] twice, p6, k2, W&T.

Row 11: P2, [Braid Right, p3] twice, Braid Right, p2, W&T.

Row 12: K2, [p6, k3] three times, p6, k1, W&T.

Row 13: P1, [Braid Left, p3] four times, Braid Left, p1, W&T.

Row 14: K1, [p6, k3] four times, p6, k2, W&T.

Row 15: P2, [Braid Right, p3] four times, Braid Right, p2, W&T.

Row 16: K2, [p6, k3] six times, p2, W&T.

Row 17: K2, p3, [Braid Left, p3] seven times, k2, W&T.

Row 18: P2, k3, [p6, k3] seven times, p3, W&T.

Row 19: K3, p3, [Braid Right, p3] seven times, k3, W&T.

Row 20: P3, k3, [p6, k3] seven times, p4, W&T.

Row 21: K4, p3, [Braid Left, p3] twice, k20, W&T.
Under & Upper Lip & Mouth Shaping

Row 22 (WS): P17, W&T.

Row 23: K to 1 st beyond W&T from 2 rows down, W&T.

Row 24: P to 1 st beyond W&T from 2 rows down, W&T.

Row 25: [K2tog-L, slip st just formed onto LH needle] 18 times, (you should be in the middle of a braid.) K3 (half of braid sts), p3, [Braid Left, p3] twice, k4, W&T.

Row 26: P4, k3, [p6, k3] twice, p3, CO 17 sts, p3, k3, [p6, k3] twice, p4, W&T– 73 sts across front.

Row 27: K4, p3, [Braid Right, p3] twice, k2, [p1, sl 1] nine times, p1, k2, p3, [Braid Right, p3] twice,

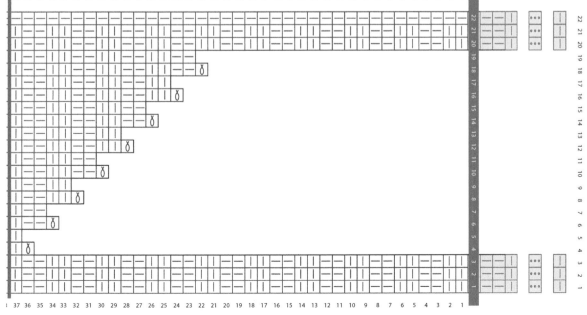

### S Hoo 5 Eyelid Shaping (Rows 69 & 70)

### S Hoo 4 Nose Bridge (Rows 51-68)

### S Hoo 3 Nose Tip (Rows 45-50)

### S Hoo 2 Upper Chin & Mouth Shaping (Rows 1-44)

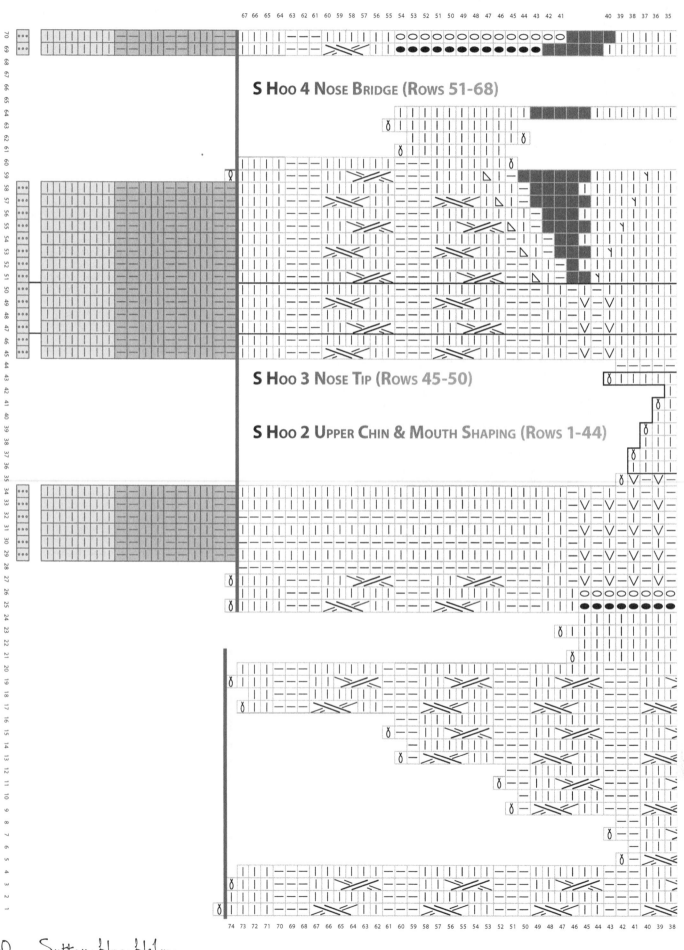

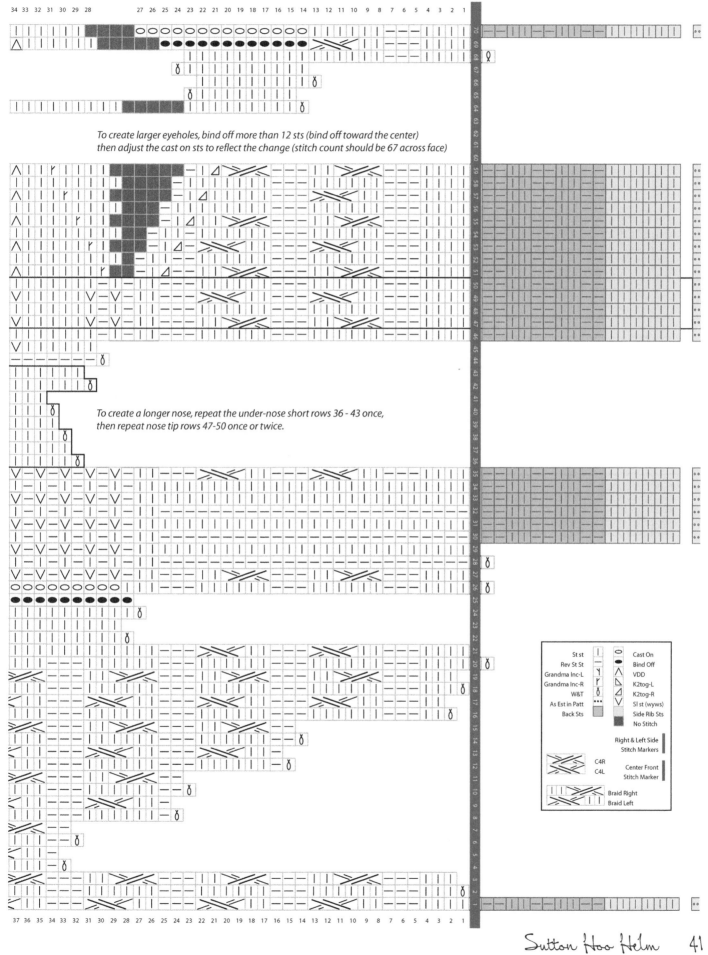

To create larger eyeholes, bind off more than 12 sts (bind off toward the center)
then adjust the cast on sts to reflect the change (stitch count should be 67 across face)

To create a longer nose, repeat the under-nose short rows 36 - 43 once,
then repeat nose tip rows 47-50 once or twice.

| | St st | | | Cast On |
| | Rev St St | | | Bind Off |
| | Grandma Inc-L | | | VDD |
| | Grandma Inc-R | | | K2tog-L |
| | W&T | | | K2tog-R |
| | As Est in Patt | | | Sl st (wyws) |
| | Back Sts | | | Side Rib Sts |
| | | | | No Stitch |

Right & Left Side
Stitch Markers

C4R
C4L

Center Front
Stitch Marker

Braid Right
Braid Left

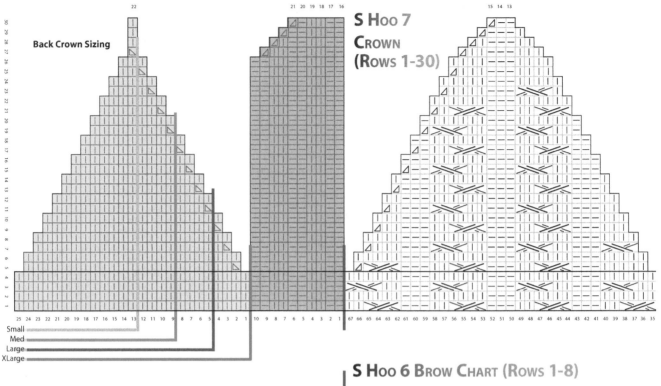

**Back Crown Sizing**

**S Hoo 7 Crown (Rows 1-30)**

Small
Med
Large
XLarge

**S Hoo 6 Brow Chart (Rows 1-8)**

k4, W&T.

Row 28: K25, p2, [k1, p1] nine times, k1, p2, k25, W&T.

Row 29: K27, [p1, sl 1] 9 times, p1, k27, sm, join second ball of A and cont with A, slipping wraps onto needle and working tog with wrapped sts as in previous rows., [p2, k2] twice, p2, k13 (17, 21, 25) to end of round. Turn work.

Rows 30, 32: (WS):, P13 (17, 21, 25), [k2, p2] twice, k2, sm, change to B, k25, p2, [k1, p1] nine times, k1, p2, k25, sm, change to A, [k2, p2] twice, k2, p13 (17, 21, 25).

Rows 31 & 33: K13 (17, 21, 25), [p2, k2] twice, p2, sm, k27, [p1, sl 1] nine times, p1, k27, sm, [p2, k2] twice, p2, k13 (17, 21, 25) sts.

Row 34: (WS):, P13 (17, 21, 25), [k2, p2] twice, k2, sm, change to B, p27, [k1, p1] nine times, k1, p27, sm, change to A, [k2, p2] twice, k2, p13 (17, 21, 25).

Row 35: K13 (17, 21, 25), [p2, k2] twice, p2, sm, k4, p3, [Braid Left, p3] twice, k2, [p1, sl 1] seven times, W&T.

Row 36 (WS): P9, W&T.
Row 37 (RS): K8, W&T.
Row 38: P7, W&T.
Row 39: K6, W&T.
Row 40: P5, W&T.
Row 41: K4, W&T.
Row 42: P7, W&T.
Row 43: K11, W&T.
Row 44 (WS) K12, W&T.

## CHART 3 NOSE TIP

Row 45 (RS): K6, sl 1, k5, [sl 1, p1] twice, k2, p3, [Braid Left, p3] twice, k4, [p2, k2] twice, p2, k13

(17, 21, 25) sts.

Rows 46, 48 & 50 (WS): P13 (17, 21, 25), [k2, p2] twice, k2, p4, k3, [p6, k3] twice, p2, k1, p1, k1, p13, k1, p1, k1, p2, k3, [p6, pk3] twice, p4, [k2, p2] twice, k2, p13 (17, 21, 25) sts.

Row 47 (RS): K13 (17, 21, 25), [p2, k2] twice, p2, k4, p3, [Braid Right, p3] twice, k2, [p1, sl 1] twice, k5, sl 1, k5, [sl 1, p1,] twice, k2, p3, [Braid Right, p3] twice, k4, [p2, k2] twice, p2, k13 (17, 21, 25) sts.

Row 49 (RS): K13 (17, 21, 25), [p2, k2] twice, p2, k4, p3, [Braid Left, p3] twice, k2, [p1, sl 1] twice, k5, sl 1, k5, [sl 1, p1,] twice, k2, p3, [Braid Left, p3] twice, k4, [p2, k2] twice, p2, k13 (17, 21, 25) sts.

## CHART 4 NOSE BRIDGE

Row 51 (RS): K13 (17, 21, 25), [p2, k2] twice, p2, k4, [p3, Braid Right] twice, p2, k2tog-R, k1, p1, GR inc, k6, VDD, k6, GL inc, p1, k1, k2tog-L, p2, [Braid Right, p3] twice, k4, [p2, k2] twice, p2, k13 (17, 21, 25) sts.

Row 52: P13 (17, 21, 25), [k2, p2] twice, k2, p4, [k3, p6] twice, k2, p2, k1, p17, k1, p2, k2, [p6, k3] twice, p4, [k2, p2] twice, k2, p13 (17, 21, 25) sts.

Continuing to work back and 10-st side rib sections as est, work across face sts as foll:

Row 53: Work to marker as est, k4, [p3, Braid Left] twice, p1, k2tog-R, k1, p1, k1, GR inc, k5, VDD, k5, GL inc, k1, p1, k1, k2tog-L, p1, [Braid Left, p3] twice, k4, work to end of row.

Row 54: Work to marker as est, p4, [k3, p6] twice, k1, p2, k1, p17, k1, p2, k1, [p6, k3] twice, p4, work to end of row.

Row 55: Work to marker as est, k4, [p3, Braid Right] twice, k2tog-R, k1, p1, k2, GR inc, k4, VDD, k4, GL inc, k2, p1, k1, k2tog-L, [Braid Right, p3]

twice, k4, work to end of row.

Row 56: Work to marker as est, p4, [k3, p6] twice, p2, k1, p17, k1, p2, [p6, k3] twice, p4, work to end of row.

Row 57: Work to marker as est, k4, p3, Braid Left, p3, k5, k2tog-R, k1, p1, k3, GR inc, k3, GL inc, k3, p1, k1, k2tog-L, k1, C4L, p3, Braid Left, p3, k4, work to end of row.

Row 58: Work to marker as est, p4, [k3, p6] twice, p1, k1, p17, k1, p1, [p6, k3] twice, p4, work to end of row.

Row 59: Work to marker as est, k4, p3, Braid Right, p3, C4R, k2tog-R, k1, p1, k4, GR inc, k2, VDD, k2, GL inc, k4, p1, k1, k2tog-L, k4, p3, Braid Right, p3, k4, W&T.

**Right Under Eye**

Row 60 (WS): P4, [k3, p6] twice, W&T.
Row 61 (RS): K8, W&T.
Row 62: P9, W&T.
Row 63: K10, W&T.
Row 64: P36, W&T.

**Left Under Eye**

Row 65: K8, W&T.
Rows 66 & 67: Rep Rows 62 & 63
Row 68: P16, k3, p4, W&T.

## CHART 5 EYELID SHAPING

Row 69: K4, p3, Braid Left, BO 12, k6, VDD, k6, BO 12, Braid Left, p3, k4, cont in patt as est to end of round.

Row 70: Work to marker as est, p4, k3, p6, CO 14, p11, CO 14, p6, k3, p4, cont in patt as est to end of round – 114 (122, 130, 138) sts.

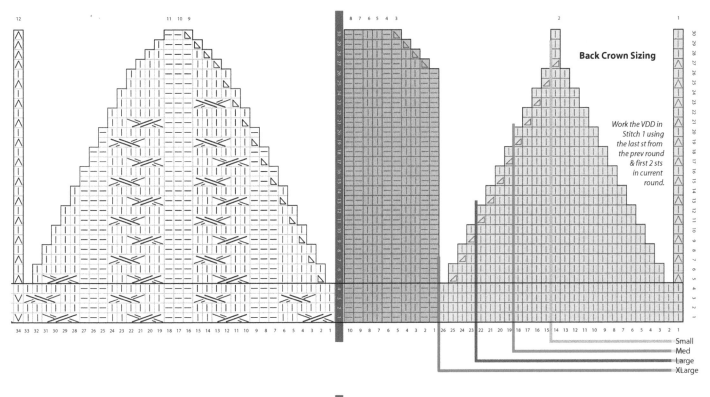

**Back Crown Sizing**

*Work the VDD in Stitch 1 using the last st from the prev round & first 2 sts in current round.*

Small
Med
Large
XLarge

## CHART 6 BROW

Row 1: K13 (17, 21, 25), [p2, k2] twice, p2, k33, sl 1, k33, [p2, k2] twice, p2, k13 (17, 21, 25).
Row 2: P13 (17, 21, 25), [k2, p2] twice, k2, p67, [k2, p2] twice, k2, p13 (17, 21, 25).
Rows 3 & 5: Sl 1, p13 (17, 21, 25), [p2, k2] twice, p2, p33, sl 1, p33, [p2, k2] twice, p2, p13 (17, 21, 25).
Rows 4 & 6: K13 (17, 21, 25), [p2, k2] twice, p2, k35, p1, k33, [p2, k2] twice, p2, k15 (19, 23, 27).
Rounds 7 & 8: Rep rnds 1 & 2. Break B.

## CHART 7 CROWN SHAPING

Round 1: K13 (17, 21, 25), [p2, k2] twice, p2, [Braid Right, p3] 3 times, Braid Right, sl 1, Braid Right [p3, Braid Right] three times, [p2, k2] p2, k13 (17, 21, 25) – 114 (122, 130, 138) sts
Round 2 and all Even Rounds: K the knit sts and P the purl sts.
Round 3: K13 (17, 21, 25), [p2, k2] twice, p2, [Braid Left, p3] 3 times, Braid Left, sl 1, Braid Left [p3, Braid Left] three times, [p2, k2] p2, k13 (17, 21, 25) – 114 (122, 130, 138) sts.
Rep Rounds 1-4 0 (1, 2, 3) times, or until pieces reaches to just above tip of ears, ending final round 1 st before end of round. Cont working Crown Chart, decreasing as directed.
Round 5: Remove marker, VDD (worked over the last st of the previous round and the first 2 sts of the current round,) k12 (16, 20, 22), k2tog-R 0 (0, 0, 1) time, [p2, k2] twice, p2, K2tog-L, k4, [p3, Braid Right] twice, p3, C4R, k1, VDD, k5, p3, [Braid Right, p3] twice, C4R, k2tog-R, [p2, k2] twice, p2, k2tog-L 0 (0, 0, 1) time, k12 (16, 20, 22)

sts – 108 (116, 124, 130) sts.
Rounds 6 and all following even rounds up to and including 26: K the knit sts and P the purl sts, stopping 1 st before VDD from prev round.
Round 7: VDD, k11 (15, 19, 20), k2tog-R 0 (0, 0, 1) times, [p2, k2] twice, p2, k2tog-L, k3, [p3, Braid Left] twice, p3, k4, VDD, C4L, p3, [Braid Right, p3] twice, k3, k2tog-R, [p2, k2] twice, p2, k2tog-L 0 (0, 0, 1) times, k11 (15, 19, 20) sts – 102 (110, 118, 122) sts.
Round 9: VDD, k10 (14, 18, 18), k2tog-R 0 (0, 0, 1) times, [p2, k2] twice, p2, k2tog-L, k2, [p3, Braid Right] twice, p3, k3, VDD, k3, p3, [Braid Right, p3] twice, k2, k2tog-R, [p2, k2] twice, p2, k2tog-L 0 (0, 0, 1) times, k10 (14, 18, 18) sts – 96 (104, 112, 114) sts.
Round 11: VDD, k9 (13, 16, 16), k2tog-R 0 (0, 0, 1) times, [p2, k2] twice, p2, k2tog-L, k1, p3, [Braid Left, p3] twice, k2, VDD, k2, p3, [Braid Left, p3] twice, k1, k2tog-R, [p2, k2] twice, p2, k2tog-L 0 (0, 0, 1) times, k9 (13, 16, 16) sts – 90 (98, 104, 106) sts.
Round 13: VDD, k8 (12, 14, 14), k2tog-R 0 (0, 1, 1) times, [p2, k2] twice, p2, k2tog-L, p3, [Braid Right, p3] twice, k1, VDD, k1, p3, [Braid Right, p3] twice, k2tog-R, [p2, k2] twice, p2, k2tog-L 0 (0, 1, 1) times, k8 (12, 14, 14) sts – 84 (92, 96, 98) sts.
Round 15: VDD, k7 (11, 12, 12), k2tog-R 0 (0, 1, 1) times, [p2, k2] twice, p2, k2tog-L, p2, [Braid Left, p3] twice, VDD, [p3, Braid Left] twice, p2, k2tog-R, [p2, k2] twice, p2, k2tog-L 0 (0, 1, 1) times, k7 (11, 12, 12) sts – 78 (86, 88, 90) sts.
Round 17: VDD, k6 (10, 10, 10), k2tog-R 0 (0, 1, 1) times, [p2, k2] twice, p2, k2tog-L, p1, Braid Right, p3, Braid Right, p2, VDD, p2, Braid Right, p3, Braid Right, p1, k2tog-R, [p2, k2] twice, p2,

k2tog-L 0 (0, 1, 1) times, k6 (10, 10, 10) sts – 72 (80, 80, 82) sts.
Round 19: VDD, k5 (8, 8, 8), k2tog-R 0 (1, 1, 1) times, [p2, k2] twice, p2, k2tog-L, Braid Left, p3, Braid Left, p1, VDD, p1, Braid Left, p3, Braid Left, k2tog-R, [p2, k2] twice, p2, k2tog-L 0 (1, 1, 1) times, k5 (8, 8, 8) sts – 66 (72, 72, 74) sts.
Round 21: VDD, k4 (6, 6, 6), k2tog-R 0 (1, 1, 1) times, [p2, k2] twice, p2, k2tog-L, k5, p3, Braid Right, VDD, Braid Right, p3, C4R, k1, k2tog-R, [p2, k2] twice, p2, k2tog-L 0 (1, 1, 1) times, k4 (6, 6, 6) sts – 60 (64, 64, 66) sts.
Round 23: VDD, k3 (4, 4, 4), k2tog-R 0 (1, 1, 1) times, [p2, k2] twice, p2, k2tog-L, C4L, p3, k5, VDD, k1, C4L, p3, k4, k2tog-R, [p2, k2] twice, p2, k2tog-L 0 (1, 1, 1) times, k3 (4, 4, 4) sts – 54 (56, 56, 58) sts.
Round 25: VDD, k2 (2, 2, 2), k2tog-R 0 (1, 1, 1) times, [p2, k2] twice, p2, k2tog-L, k3, p3, k4, VDD, k4, p3, k3, k2tog-R, [p2, k2] twice, p2, k2tog-L 0 (1, 1, 1) times, k2 (2, 2, 2) sts – 48 (48, 48, 50) sts
Round 27: VDD, k1 (k2tog-R, k2tog-R, k2tog-R), k2tog-L, [k2, p2] twice, k2tog-L, k2, p3, k3, VDD, k3, p3, k2, k2tog-R, [p2, k2] twice, k2tog-R, k1 (k2tog-L, k2tog-L, k2tog-L),– 36 (38, 38, 38) sts.
Round 28: K2 (2, 2, 2), k2tog-L, k1, p2, k2, k2tog-L, k1, p3, k2, VDD, k2, p3, k1, k2tog-R, p2, k2, p2, k1, k2tog-R, k1 (1, 1, 1) sts – 32 (34, 34, 34) sts.
Round 29: K2 (2, 2, 2), k2tog-L, p2, k2, p2, k2tog-L, p3, k1, VDD, k1, p3, k2tog-R, p2, k2, p2, k2tog-R, k1 (1, 1, 1) sts – 26 (28, 28, 28) sts.
Round 30: K2 (2, 2, 2), k2tog-L, p1, k2, p2, k2tog-L, p2, VDD, k2tog-R, p2, k2, p1, k2tog-R, k1 (1, 1, 1) sts – 20 (22, 22, 22) sts.

A simple, satisfying, and easy-traveling knit, the Lady Margaret Scarf is dressed up with high-contrast decorative chain embroidery.
*Background: Canterbury Cathedral Interior*
*Lady Margaret Scarf modeled by Debra Schlekewy, knit by Annie Modesitt*

# Lady Margaret Scarf

Influenced by Moorish motifs first seen during the crusades, blackwork embroidery became a mainstay of Tudor and Stuart England.

Catherine of Aragon, the first wife of Henry VIII, is widely considered to have popularized Blackwork Embroidery when she arrived from Spain.

However, there is strong evidence that Blackwork Embroidery – which can be defined in simple terms as the use of black silk thread on a fine linen or cotton background – was introduced in England during the time of the crusades.

I feel the rise of Blackwork during the Tudor and Stuart eras is fitting in a time of strong women and stark choices.

Reversing the established fiber choices, I used black merino wool yarn on a gridded silk background to recreate the strong geometric effect of Lady Margaret Beaufort's veil in the portrait.

The lines are simplified to accommodate the Decorative Chain Embroidery technique, which is not as fine as traditional Blackwork Embroidery.

Alternatively, the decorative chain embroidery could be magnificent if worked using a long-repeat variegated yarn.

*(possibly)* **Lady Margaret Beaufort**
*mother of Henry VII, grandmother of Henry VIII,*
*Margaret, and Mary Tudor,*
**c. 1443**

## LADY MARGARET SCARF INFO

| | |
|---|---|
| One Size | 12" x 64" |
| Skill Level | K 3 Intermediate |
| Fiber A | Henry's Attic, Silk Avalanche (275yds/251m 3.5oz/100gr) Natural Off White, 1 skein |
| Fiber B | Muench Merino Soft (186yds/170m 1.75oz/50gr) 15 Black, 1 ball |
| Gauge | 19 sts x 23 rows = 4"/20cm using needle size: 6US/4mm |
| Needles | Size 6US/4mm |
| Notions | Darning needle, waste yarn, size GUS/4mm crochet hook |

## LADY MARGARET SCARF STITCHES

St st – Stockinette Stitch
Rev St st – Reverse St st
Sl st wyws – Slip st with yarn to the wrong side
Sl st wyrs – Slip st with yarn to the right side

## LADY MARGARET SCARF TECHNIQUES

Provisional Cast On
DKSS Edge – Double Knit Slip Stitch Edge
Decorative Chain Embroidery
I-Cord Bind Off

*See Special Techniques, page 116, for full explanations on how to work the stitches and techniques listed above.*

## TEXTURE CHART

Row 1 (RS): K1, sl 1 wyrs, k1 (DKSS edge), p2, [k7, sl 1] five times, k7, p2, DKSS edge.
Row 2 (WS): Sl 1 wyws, k1, sl 1 wyws (DKSS edge), k2, p to last 5 sts, k2, DKSS edge.
Rows 3-9: Rep Rows 1 & 2 three times more, then work Row 1 once more.
Row 10 (WS): DKSS edge, k9, p1, [k7, p 1] four times, k9 DKSS edge.

# LADY MARGARET SCARF

## CAST ON

With waste yarn and using any provisional cast on method (see Special Techniques, page 116, CO 57 sts. With A, purl 1 row.

## SCARF BODY

Working from written or charted instructions as you prefer, work the 10 rows of Texture Chart 36 times, 360 rows total worked, (36 bands separated by rev st st rows) then work rows 1-8 once more.

## I CORD BIND OFF

Preparation Insert needle into first 2 sts on needle through the back loop and slip them together onto the right needle. Return them to the left needle, reversing their order, by 'backing' them on (the tips of both needles will be pointing in the same direction).

Bind Off Row: K3, slip 3 sts back onto left needle. [K2, k2tog-L, slip 3 sts back onto left needle] rep until 3 sts rem, k3tog-L.

Return to provisional cast on sts and carefully slip them onto needle. With Right Side of work facing, work I-Cord Bind Off as before.

Before embroidering the scarf, steam block the entire piece thoroughly.

## EMBROIDERY

Using B, the crochet hook and the Decorative Chain Embroidery technique, (see Special Techniques, page 116) work along the entire length of the scarf 6 times, following the charted diagram and repeating the section between the dashed lines.

Work the outer edge lines (1 & 2) first, then work the center zig-zag motif a total of 4 times, creating the lattice and loop design. Base the embroidery lines on the grid pattern established in the scarf.

## TIPS

When working the embroidery, a large hoop can be helpful, but will need to be moved frequently as you work along the length of the scarf. Don't strive for perfection (it's a hand made piece, after all!) but try to work evenly and in a relaxed manner.

It's VERY useful to practice the technique on a swatch in order to feel comfortable.

**The embroidery is based on a knitted grid pattern (shown here in wool).**

## LADY MARGARET SCARF TEXTURE CHART

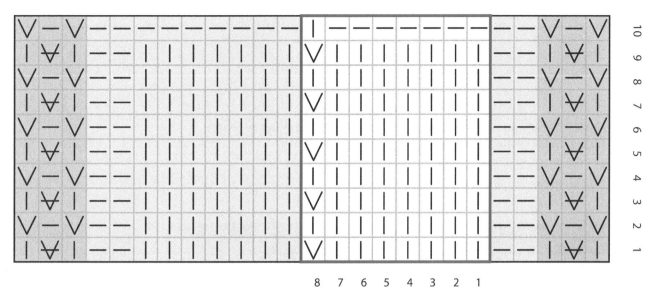

| St st | $\vert$ |
| Rev St St | $-$ |
| Sl 1 wyws | $\vee$ |
| Sl 1 wyrs | $\curlyvee$ |

## LADY MARGARET SCARF EMBROIDERY CHART

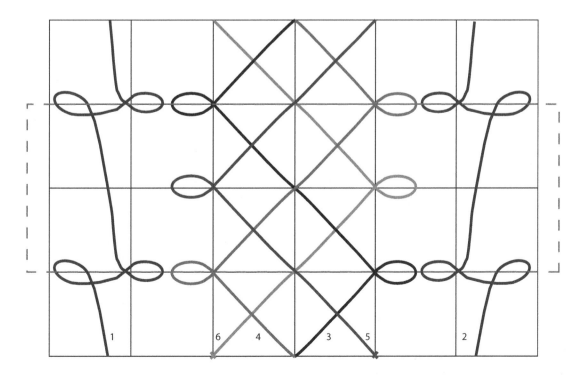

**The Woodstock Tunic can be knit as long as you like, or kept short to match Prince Edward's own styling choices (shield optional).**

*Background: Canterbury Cathedral Interior Composite*

*Woodstock Tunic modeled by Ellis Norris, knit by Annie Modesitt*

Garment Photo: Jen Simonson, Background Photo: Annie Modesitt

# Woodstock Tunic

A short garment based on Edward of Woodstock's battle tunic, wear this as a mini dress, or as a long pullover.

In the *Oxford Dictionary of National Biography*, historian Richard Barber described Edward of Woodville as attracting *"relatively little attention from serious historians, but [he] figures largely in popular history."*

Edward, son of King Edward III and father of King Richard II, never reigned as monarch, dying a week before his 46th birthday.

Handsome, glamorous, chivalrous toward his peers, but merciless to those in the lower classes, Edward of Woodstock is a complex figure who might be easily romanticized.

The garment I've based on his tunic surcoat is quartered to reflect the elements of Edward's shield.

Edward of Woodstock's Shield
French Fleur de Lys & English Lions

The Plantagenet lions *(in English red)* and the fleur de lys *(in French blue)* are worked using the jacquard technique, which creates subtle images in the fabric texture by juxtaposing knit and purl stitches.

Edward "The Black Prince" Funeral Effigy
Canterbury Cathedral c. 1380

Photo composite ©Annie Modesitt

## WOODSTOCK TUNIC INFORMATION

| | |
|---|---|
| To Fit Bust | 34 (38, 42, 46, 50, 54, 58)"/86.5 (97, 107, 117.5, 127.5, 138, 148) cm |
| Finished Bust | 38 (42, 46, 50, 54, 58, 62)"/97 (107, 117.5, 127.5, 138, 148, 158) cm |
| Length | 30 (31, 32, 33, 34, 35, 36)"/76.5 (79, 81.5, 84, 86.5, 89.5, 92) cm |
| Skill Level | K 3 Intermediate |
| Fiber | Berroco, Pure Merino Chine (92yds/84m 1.75oz/50gr) Color A, 8656 Yelloise 4 (5, 7, 8, 11, 13) skeins Color B, 8651 Bronge 3 (5, 6, 7, 9, 12) skeins |
| Gauge | 20 sts x 32 rows = 4"/10cm in St st using needle size 7US/4.5mm |
| Needles | 6US/4mm & 7US/4.5mm 24" circ |

## WOODSTOCK TUNIC STITCHES

St st – Stockinette Stitch
Rev St st — Reverse St st

## WOODSTOCK TUNIC TECHNIQUES

PU&K – Pick Up And Knit
Jacquard Knitting
*Tip: When knitting into a purl stitch or purling into a knit stitch while working one of the jacquard motifs in this garment, twist the stitch (work into the back if you usually work into the front and vice versa) to make the motif stand out more clearly.*

*See Special Techniques, page 116, for full explanations on how to work the stitches and techniques listed above.*

# WOODSTOCK TUNIC

## FRONT

With smaller needles & color A, cast on 48 (52, 58, 62, 68, 72, 78) sts, then with color B cast on 48 (52, 58, 62, 68, 72, 78) sts. These are the 96 (104, 116, 124, 136, 144, 156) front hem stitches.

Beg with a WS row and larger needles, Establish rib as foll

WS Rows: With B, (p1, k2, p1) 12 (13, 15, 16, 17, 18, 20) times, change to A & twist colors at the WS of the work to avoid a hole, (p1, k2, p1) rep to end.
RS Rows: With A (k1, p2, k1) 12 (13, 15, 16, 17, 18, 20) times, change to B & twist colors at the WS of the work to avoid a hole, (k1, p2, k1) rep to end.

Cont in ribbing as est, changing colors in the center, crossing the strands and keeping the twist to the WS of the work, for a total of 24 rows, end with a WS row.

Switch to stockinette stitch (knit all sts on the RS, purl all sts on the WS) changing colors at the cen-

ter point as est, for a total of 5 (5, 7, 7, 9, 11, 13) rows, end with a WS row.

## FIRST JACQUARD MOTIF BAND

Next Row (RS): Knit 0 (2, 5, 7, 10, 12, 15) sts, place marker (pm). Cont with A, work row 1 of Fleur de Lys chart 3 times across next 48 sts, pm, k0 (2, 5, 7, 10, 12, 15) sts. Change color as prev est. Cont with B, k0 (2, 5, 7, 10, 12, 15) sts, pm, work row 1 of Lion chart across next 48 sts, pm, k0 (2, 5, 7, 10, 12, 15) sts

Next Row (WS): Purl to first marker, beg with stitch 48 and working back across row 2 of Lion Chart work to next marker, p to next marker, changing colors in center as established p0 (2, 5, 7, 10, 12, 15) sts, beg with stitch 16 and working back across row 2 of Fleur de Lys chart, rep 3 times to next marker, purl to end.

Cont working in charts as est, working 0 (2, 5, 7, 10, 12, 15) sts on either side of charts in St st, until all 24 rows of each chart have been worked.

Work 2 (4, 4, 4, 6, 8, 8) rows in St st, changing colors as prev est.

## SECOND JACQUARD MOTIF BAND

Next Row (RS): Knit 8 (10, 13, 15, 18, 20, 23) sts, work row 1 of Fleur de Lys chart 2 times across next 32 sts, work to center point and change color as prev est. Cont with B, work to marker, work row 1 of Lion chart across next 48 sts, work to end of row.

Next Row (WS): Purl to marker, work Lion Chart across next 48 sts, work to center point and change colors, p8 (10, 13, 15, 18, 20, 23) sts, work Fleur de Lys chart two times, purl to end.

Cont working in charts as est, working sts on either side of charts in St st, until all 24 rows of each chart have been worked.

Work 2 (4, 4, 4, 6, 8, 8) rows in St st, changing colors as prev est.

## THIRD JACQUARD MOTIF BAND

Repeat First Motif Band.

## FOURTH JACQUARD MOTIF BAND

Next Row (RS): Change to color B and work to first marker. Work Row 1 of Lion Chart across next 48 sts, work to center point and change to color A and work to next marker. Work Row 1 of Fleur de Lys chart three times to next marker, knit to end of row.

Next Row (WS): With color A purl to marker, work Fleur de Lys Chart three times across next 48 sts, work to center point and change colors as est. With color B work to marker, work Lion chart across next 48 sts, work to end of row.

Cont working in charts as est, working sts on either side of charts in St st, until all 24 rows of each chart have been worked.

Work 2 (4, 4, 4, 6, 8, 8) rows in St st, changing colors as prev est.

## WOODSTOCK LION CHART

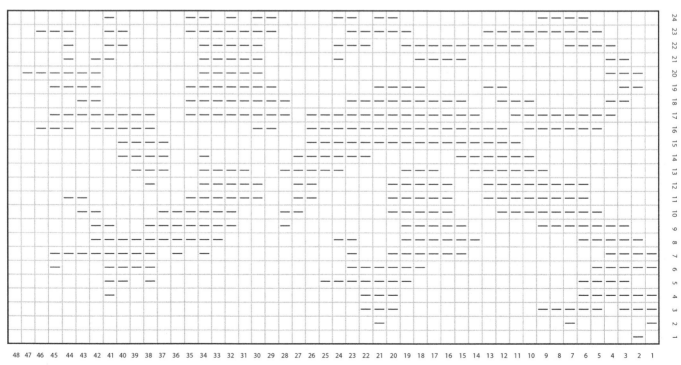

## Fifth Jacquard Motif Band

Next Row (RS): Work to marker, then work row 1 of Lion chart across next 48 sts, work to center point & change colors. Knit 8 (10, 13, 15, 18, 20, 23) sts, work row 1 of Fleur de Lys chart two times across next 32 sts, work to end of row.

Next Row (WS): Purl 8 (10, 13, 15, 18, 20, 23) sts, work Fleur de Lys chart two times, purl to center point, change colors. Purl to marker, work Lion Chart across next 48 sts, work to end of row.

Cont working in charts as est, working sts on either side of charts in St st, until all 24 rows of each chart have been worked.

Work 2 (4, 4, 4, 6, 8, 8) rows in St st, changing colorscolors as prev est.

## Sixth Jacquard Motif Band

Repeat Fourth Motif Band, then work 24 (24, 24, 24, 24, 24, 24) rows in St st, changing colors as prev est.

AND AT THE SAME TIME, when work meas 40½ (41, 41½, 42, 43, 43½, 44½)"/103.5 (104.5, 106, 107, 109.5, 111, 113.5) cm from cast on row, begin armhole shaping as foll, cont in charted patt in rem body sts.

## Armhole Shaping

Bind off 2 (2, 2, 2, 4, 4, 6) sts at start of next 2 rows. Then BO 2 (3, 4, 4, 5, 6, 6) sts at start of next 4 rows. Then BO 1 st at start of next 4 (8, 8, 8, 12, 16, 16) times rows – 80 (80, 88, 96, 96, 96, 104) sts rem.

## Neck Shaping

Bind off center 20 (20, 22, 22, 22, 22, 22) sts, [10 (10, 11, 11, 11, 11, 11) sts in each color], then BO3 (3, 3, 3, 3, 3, 3) sts every other row at neck edge 4 times, then BO 1 st every 4th row 2 (2, 5, 5, 5, 5, 5) times

Work as est, cont in St st once all rows of jacquard charts are finished. When neck depth meas 3½ (4, 4½, 5, 5, 5, 5)"/9 (10, 11.5, 13, 13, 13, 13) cm [armhole dept should meas 9½ (10, 10½, 11, 11, 11½, 11½)"/24 (25.5, 27, 28, 28, 29.5, 29.5) cm] slip rem 16 (16, 16, 20, 20, 20, 24) sts at each shoulder to a stitch holder to work later.

## BACK

With smaller needles & color A, cast on 48 (52, 58, 62, 68, 72, 78) sts, then with color B cast on 48 (52, 58, 62, 68, 72, 78) sts. These are the 96 (104, 116, 124, 136, 144, 156) back stitches.

## Ribbing

Beg with a WS row and larger needles, Establish rib as foll:

WS Rows: With B, (p1, k2, p1) 12 (13, 15, 16, 17, 18, 20) times, change to A & twist colors at the WS of the work to avoid a hole, (p1, k2, p1) rep to end. RS Rows: With A (k1, p2, k1) 12 (13, 15, 16, 17, 18, 20) times, change to B & twist colors at the WS of the work to avoid a hole, (k1, p2, k1) rep to end. Cont in ribbing as est, changing colors in the center, crossing the strands and keeping the twist to the WS of the work, for a total of 24 rows. Change to larger needles and cont in rib as est until length matches color change point on the Front.

Cont in rib as est, change colors so sts that had been worked in color A are now worked in color B and vice versa. Cont in ribbing until same distance as front to armhole bind off from cast on. End with a WS row.

## Back Armhole Shaping

Shape armholes as for Front Work even until armhole

depth is even with Front.

## Joining Shoulders

Slip 16 (16, 16, 20, 20, 20, 24) Right Front shoulder sts to needle and using a 3rd needle, join Right shoulder using a 3-needle bind off. Repeat for Left Shoulder.

Bind off rem 48 (48, 56, 56, 56, 56, 56) Back neck sts

## SLEEVE

With smaller needles & color A, cast on 36 (42, 42, 48, 48, 48, 48) sts. Join work, placing a marker to note the start of round.

Next Round: (K1, p2, k1) rep to end of round, the marker should sit between two knit stitches. Cont in ribbing as est for a total of 6"/15.5cm. Change to larger needles.

## Lower Sleeve

Work 2 rounds in garter (knit 1 round, purl 1 round)

Next Round: Beg with stitch 1, work row 1 of Lower Sleeve chart around all stitches.

Cont in patt as est, inc by working a Kfb on either side of the marker (first and last sts of the round) every other round, increasing 2 sts every 4 rounds 30 (30, 33, 30, 30, 33, 33) times.

Work new sts into charted pattern and AT THE SAME TIME, when sleeve meas 4½ (4¾, 5, 5, 5½, 5¾, 5¾)"/11.5 (12, 13, 13, 14, 14.5, 14.5) cm from top of cuff, or desired lower sleeve length, work 2 rounds in garter stitch.

## Upper Sleeve

Change to color B and work 2 rounds of garter stitch, then begin working Upper Sleeve Chart, matching placement of stitch number in Upper Sleeve Chart to Lower Sleeve Chart. Cont inc as est in lower sleeve section until there are a total of 96 (102, 108, 108, 108, 114, 114) sts. Work even until sleeve meas 21 (22, 23, 23, 24, 25, 25)"/53.5 (56, 58.5, 58.5, 61, 64, 64) cm from cast on edge (including 6" of cuff), or desired length. End with a WS row.

## Cap Shaping

BO 4 (4, 4, 4, 8, 8, 12) sts, work to marker. Turn work & BO 4 (4, 4, 4, 8, 8, 12) sts, work back in charted patt across row –88 (94, 100, 100, 92, 98, 90) sts rem.

Cont to work back and forth in charted patt, shape cap sleeve as foll:

BO 3 at start of every row 24 (26, 28, 28, 26, 28, 26) times–16 (16, 16, 16, 14, 14, 12) sts

Work 2 (2, 2, 2, 4, 4, 2) rows even with no decreasing, then BO 1 st at start of every row 4 times. BO rem 12 (12, 12, 12, 10, 10, 8) sts.

## FINISHING

Steam block pieces. Baste sleeve into armscye and sew in place.

## Neck

With smaller circular needle, color B and RS facing, PU&K 20 (20, 22, 22, 22, 22, 22) sts across the center Back neck, PU&K 42 (48, 54, 60, 60, 60, 60) sts down left neck edge, PU&K 20 (20, 22, 22, 22, 22, 22) sts across the center front, PU&K 42 (48, 54, 60, 60, 60, 60) sts up right neck edge –82 (88, 98, 104, 104, 104, 104) sts. Knit all stitches a total of 16 rounds, then bind off LOOSELY using larger needle. Steam block neck edge, allowing it to roll.

Weave in ends.

## WOODSTOCK FLEUR DE LYS CHART

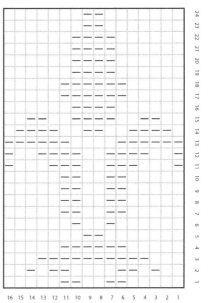

| St st | |
| Rev St st | — |

## WOODSTOCK LOWER SLEEVE CHART

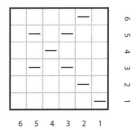

## WOODSTOCK UPPER SLEEVE CHART

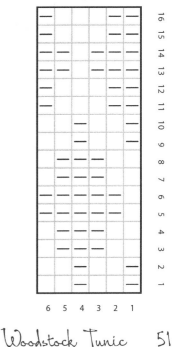

## WOODSTOCK SLEEVE SCHEMATIC

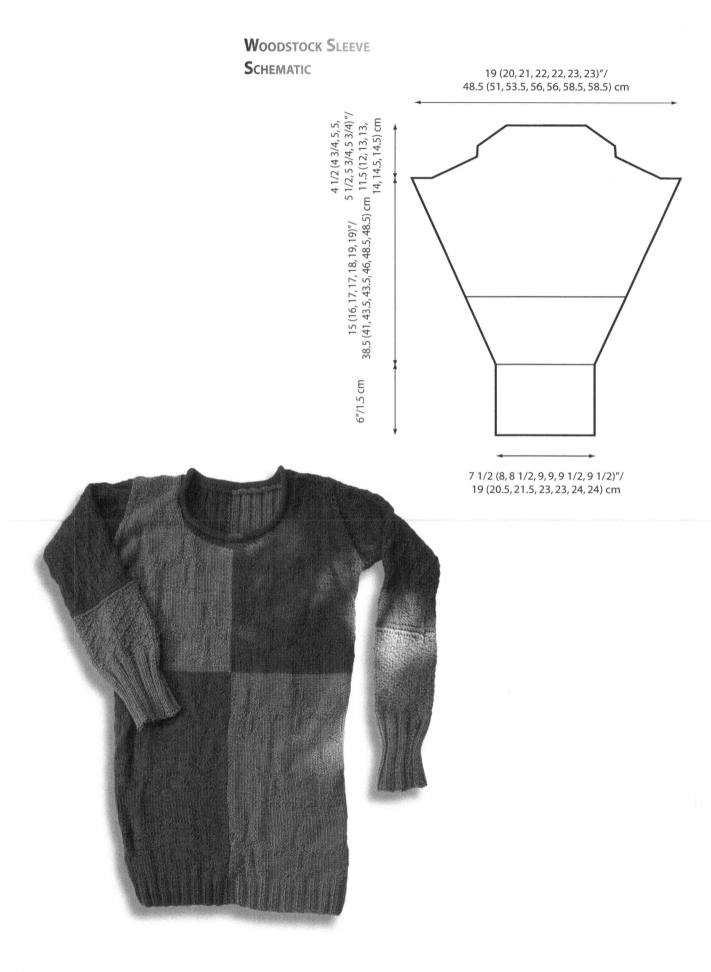

19 (20, 21, 22, 22, 23, 23)"/
48.5 (51, 53.5, 56, 56, 58.5, 58.5) cm

4 1/2 (4 3/4, 4, 5, 5,
5 1/2, 5 3/4, 5 3/4)"/
11.5 (12, 13, 13,
14, 14.5, 14.5) cm

15 (16, 17, 17, 18, 19, 19)"/
38.5 (41, 43.5, 43.5, 46, 48.5, 48.5) cm

6"/1.5 cm

7 1/2 (8, 8 1/2, 9, 9, 9 1/2, 9 1/2)"/
19 (20.5, 21.5, 23, 23, 24, 24) cm

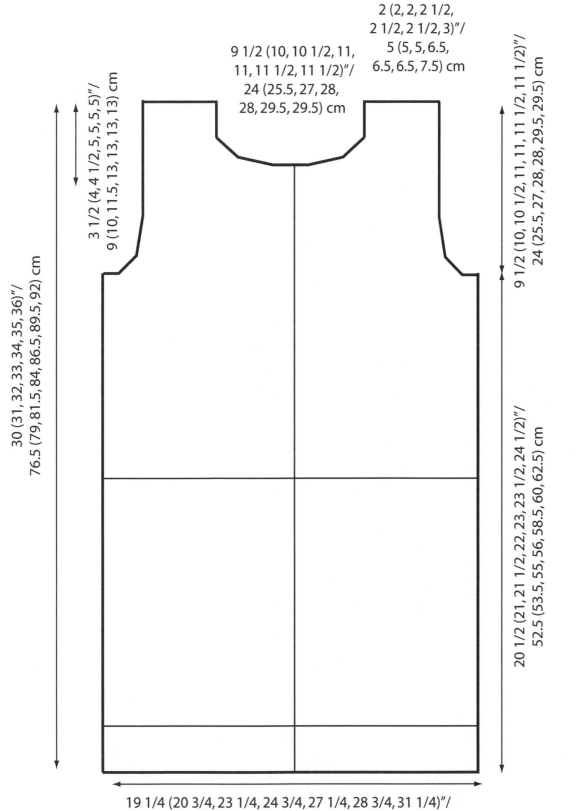

2 (2, 2, 2 1/2,
2 1/2, 2 1/2, 3)"/
5 (5, 5, 6.5,
6.5, 6.5, 7.5) cm

9 1/2 (10, 10 1/2, 11,
11, 11 1/2, 11 1/2)"/
24 (25.5, 27, 28,
28, 29.5, 29.5) cm

3 1/2 (4, 4 1/2, 5, 5, 5, 5)"/
9 (10, 11.5, 13, 13, 13, 13) cm

9 1/2 (10, 10 1/2, 11, 11, 11, 11 1/2, 11 1/2)"/
24 (25.5, 27, 28, 28, 29.5, 29.5) cm

30 (31, 32, 33, 34, 35, 36)"/
76.5 (79, 81.5, 84, 86.5, 89.5, 92) cm

20 1/2 (21, 21 1/2, 22, 23, 23 1/2, 24 1/2)"/
52.5 (53.5, 55, 56, 58.5, 60, 62.5) cm

19 1/4 (20 3/4, 23 1/4, 24 3/4, 27 1/4, 28 3/4, 31 1/4)"/
49 (53, 59.5, 63, 69.5, 73.5, 79.5) cm

The Black Prince Hood is a challenging and fun knit, excellent for cold winters or an Autumn Renaissance Faire.

*Background: Canterbury Cathedral Chapel Interior*

*Black Prince Hood modeled by Hannah Landy, knit by Annie Modesitt*

# Black Prince Hood

*A fitted hood based on the funeral effigy of Edward of Woodstock, Prince of Wales, June 1330 – June 1376*

On a trip to Canterbury Cathedral I saw the Black Prince's Funeral Effigy in person, and recreating his hood as a knit garment became a holy grail for me – a test of wills – a challenge.

And I am not one to ignore a challenge!

My goal, as it is with all my patterns, was to make a garment that is actually **knittable** (by someone other than myself!)

To that end, I knew that it was necessary to simplify the sideband of the helmet, and reduce the crown to a stylized cabled wreath to represent the battle crown.

Begun at the jawline and worked to the tip, the forehead stitches are bound off with a decorative I-Cord technique.

Finally, the collar is picked up and knit down toward the chest, with a center front gusset added to make it a more loose-fitting and wearable garment.

After all, one must be able to move when one is fighting for England!

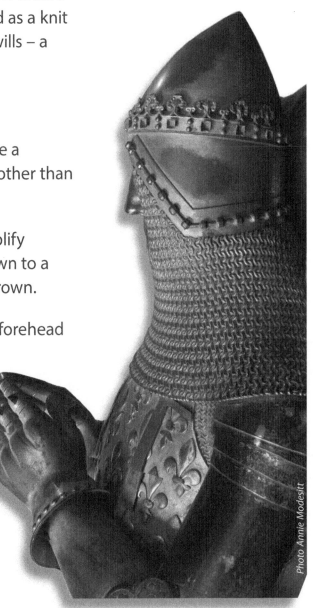

*Photo Annie Modesitt*

**Black Prince Funeral Effigy Detail**
*Canterbury Cathedral*

## BLACK PRINCE HOOD INFORMATION

| | |
|---|---|
| To fit Head | 18 (21½, 23, 26½)"/<br>45 (55, 60, 70) cm |
| Finished Circ | 20 (24, 26, 30)"/<br>51.3 (61.5, 66.7, 76.9) cm |
| Skill Level | K 3 Intermediate |
| Notions | Waste yarn (for provisional cast on), 14 (16, 17, 19 st markers, dpns for hat closure (optional) |
| Fiber | Berroco, Pure Merino Chine (92yds/84m 1.75oz/50gr) per skein 8656 Yelloise, 2 (3, 3, 4) balls |
| Gauge | 18 sts x 28 rows = 4"/10cm over St st on Size 7 US/4.5mm needles. |
| Needles | Size 7 US/4.5mm 24" circ needles (additional needles sizes 8, 9 & 10 circs) |

## BLACK PRINCE HOOD STITCHES

St st – Stockinette Stitch
Rev St st – Reverse St st
Sl st wyws – Slip st with yarn to the wrong side
Sl st wyrs – Slip st with yarn to the right side
CO – Cast On
K2tog-R – Knit 2 tog with a right slant
K2tog-L – Knit 2 tog with a left slant
GR Inc – Grandma Right Increase
GL Inc – Grandma Left Increase
VDD – Vertical Double Decrease

## BLACK PRINCE HOOD TECHNIQUES

DKSS – Double Knit Slip Stitch Edge
C4R – Cable 4 Right
C4L – Cable 4 Left
C3R – Cable 3 Right
C3L – Cable 3 Left

*See Special Techniques, page 116, for full explanations on how to work the stitches and techniques listed above*

## SIDEBAND TEXT

Row 1 (RS): DKSS RS edge, k11 (15, 15, 19) sts, pm, k4, p2, pm, k24 (24, 32, 32) sts, pm, p2, k4, pm, k11 (15, 15, 19) sts, DKSS RS edge.
Row 2 (WS): DKSS WS edge, k11 (15, 15, 19) sts, sm, p4, k2, sm, p24 (24, 32, 32) sts, sm, k2, p4, sm, k11 (15, 15, 19) sts, DKSS WS edge.
Row 3 (RS): DKSS RS edge, k to 2 sts before next marker, k2tog-R, sm, C4L, p2, sm, GR Inc, k to 1 st before next marker, GL Inc, sm, p2, C4R, sm, k2tog-L, k to last 3 sts, DKSS RS edge.
Rows 4 & 6 (WS): DKSS WS edge, k to marker, sm, p4, k2, p to next marker, sm, k2, p4, sm, k to last 3 sts, DKSS WS edge.
Row 5 (RS): DKSS RS edge, k to 2 sts before marker, k2tog-R, sm, k4, p2, sm, GR Inc, k 1 st before next marker, GL Inc, sm, p2, k4, sm, k2tog-L, k to last 3 sts, DKSS RS edge.
Rep last 4 rows until no sts rem between DKSS edge and cable (see Hood Main Chart for clarification.)

## BLACK PRINCE HOOD

### SIDEBAND

Using any provisional cast on & smallest needles, CO 64 (72, 80, 88) sts. Join working yarn.

Working from written instructions or following Sideband Chart as you prefer, work until no sts rem between DKSS edge and side cable (see Hood Main Chart for clarification) – total 22 (30, 30, 38) rows from cast on

End with Row 6 (WS row after a non-cable RS row.)

*Note: Because each dec has an accompanying inc, the stitch count remains the same.*

### CROWN

Row 1 (RS): K1, sl 1 wyrs, k2tog-R, remove

marker, C4L, p2, remove marker, GR Inc, k to 1 st before next marker, GL Inc, remove marker, p2, C4R, remove marker, k2tog-L, sl 1 wyrs, k1.
Row 2 (WS): Sl 1 wyws, k1, p5, k2, p until 9 sts rem, k2, p5, k1, sl 1 wyws.
Row 3 (RS): K2tog-L, k5, [p2, k6] rep to last 9 sts, end p2, k5, k2tog-R.
Row 4 (WS): [p6, k2] rep to last 6 sts, p6.

### FOREHEAD CAST ON

Cont on WS row, with a piece of waste yarn provisionally cast on 18 (26, 26, 34) sts onto the end of the row- 80 (96, 104, 120) sts. Turn work. Change to a circ needle and join to begin working in the round

Next Round (RS): Beg with last prov cast on, beg rnd thus: [p2, k6] 2 (3, 3, 4) times, p1, pm.
You should now be at the right edge of the work (the upper right edge of the face opening).

Round 5: [P1, C3R, C3L, p1] around.
Round 6: [P1, k6, p1] around.

### TIP

Working from written instructions or following Tip Chart as you prefer, finish top of hat then return and work the forehead sts. **FOREHEAD**

Return to provisional CO row at top of face, carefully undo and slip 18 (26, 26, 34) sts onto smallest needles. Position work so that hood is upside down and RS of work is facing you.

Beg at upper Right corner of the face (from the wearer's perspective), PU and slip 2 sts from along the DKSS edge onto LH needle.

Join a strand of yarn, [k2, k2-togL, slip 3 sts back to LH needle] rep across all forehead sts until 3 sts rem. K3tog-L Draw tail through work from RS to WS of work at point where DKSS edge meets the cable. Weave in yarn end to WS of work.

### NECK

Return to original provisional CO row, undo & slip 64 (72, 80, 88) sts onto smallest needles, arrange work so that RS is facing.

Next Row: DKSS edge, GR Inc, k to last 4 sts, GL Inc, DKSS edge.
Rep last row, (working DKSS edge as est on RS and WS rows) until there are 84 (96, 108, 120) sts on needle, then work even in garter for 4 rows, working DKSS edge as est.

**Black Prince Hood worn down as a collar.**

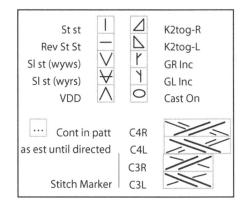

| | | | |
|---|---|---|---|
| St st | I | ◁ | K2tog-R |
| Rev St St | — | ▷ | K2tog-L |
| Sl st (wyws) | V | Y | GR Inc |
| Sl st (wyrs) | A | Y | GL Inc |
| VDD | Λ | O | Cast On |
| ⋯ Cont in patt as est until directed | | | C4R |
| | | | C4L |
| | | | C3R |
| Stitch Marker | | | C3L |

**BLACK PRINCE HOOD SIDEBAND CHARTS**

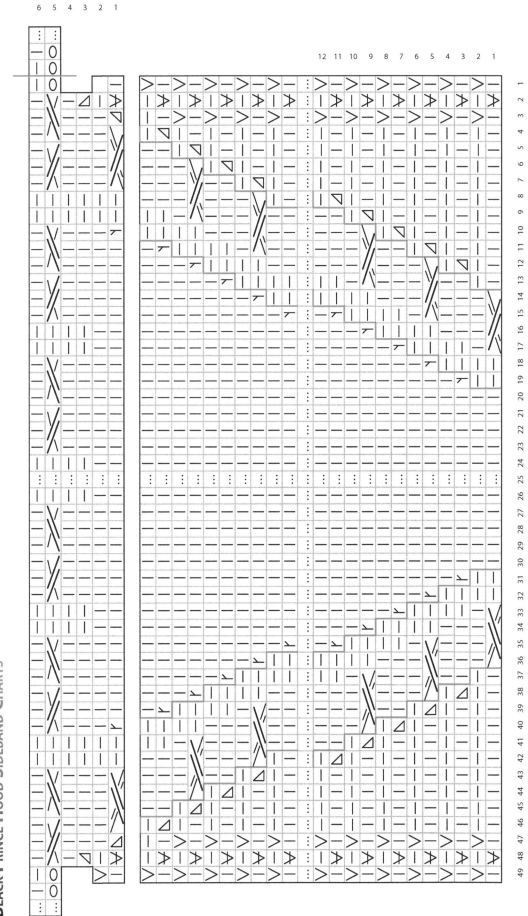

## COLLAR

Round 1 (RS): Change to a circ needle in next larger needle size. K to 3 sts before end of round, pm, knit to end of round, join.
Round 2: P to last 6 sts, k6.
Round 3: K to last 6 sts, C6L.
Round 4: Rep Round 2.
Round 5: K to last 6 sts, k3, YO, k3.
Round 6: P to last 7 sts, k3, YO, p1, YO, k3.
Round 7: K to last 9 sts, k3, YO, k3, YO, k3.
Round 8: P to last 11 sts, k3, YO, p5, YO, k3
Cont in this manner, creating an increase gusset at the center front by working at YO at beg and end of the center gusset section in every round.

At the same time, every 20 rnds (10 garter ridges) move up 1 needle size until you reach the largest size needle required for pattern. Cont working until in this manner, inc 2 sts every rnd, until hood collar reaches 6" / 15cm from chin edge, or desired length. Your final stitch count will vary depending on how deep you would like your collar to be.

Next 4 Rounds: Knit.

Loosely bind off all sts. Weave in ends, steam block piece.

**BLACK PRINCE HOOD CROWN CHART**

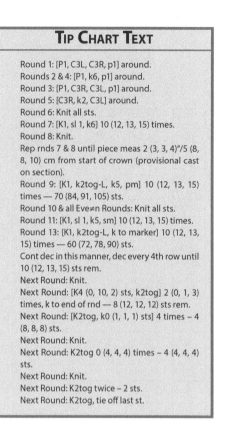
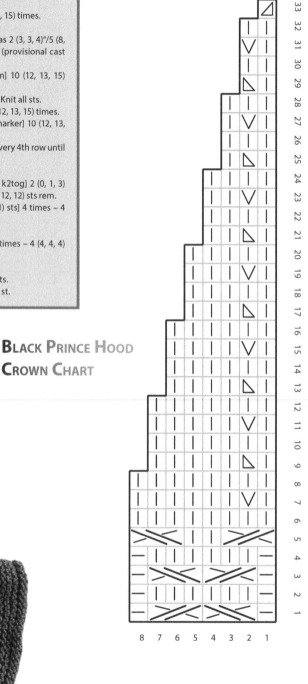

**Facing page: the Black Prince Hood in process.**

Unknown man
(formerly thought to be Charles Howard)
c. 1625

James 1st of England
and 6th of Scotland at 8
c. 1574

The Gripsholm Portrait
(though to be
Elizabeth I of England)
c. 1563

# Renaissance
## 1526-1625

Portrait thought to be of Anne Boleyn
(probably a copy of an earlier image)
c. 1536

Pembroke Jacket

Gloriana Jacket

Falkland Skirt

Admiral Anja Hat

Nottingham Hoyle Ruff

It is little wonder that we tend to romanticize the gorgeousness of the Tudor and Stuart courts.

This era, resplendent with color, jewels, and metallic detail, was replaced by a severely puritanical period of colorless dark neutrals and plain white detail.

This explosion of wealth and new ideas is labeled the English Renaissance. Fashion details of this period include slashing, puffing, intricate needlework, & entirely unnatural silhouettes. Fashions in the British Isles walked a line between the stark imprisioning garb worn in Spain & the looser, more natural French styles, two strong contemporary fashion influences.

**The structure of the Pembroke Jacket is created in part by the use of single and double crochet stitches, which are firmer than knit stitches.**
*Background: Canterbury Cathedral Interior*
*Pembroke Jacket modeled by Hannah Landy, crocheted by Annie Modesitt*

# Pembroke Jacket

Well known as the second wife of Henry VIII, Anne was created Marquess of Pembroke by Henry before their marriage.

Few women have been as vilified, romanticized, and misunderstood as Anne Boleyn.

Ambition, always unseemly in a woman of the Tudor era, was Anne's most powerful and dangerous quality.

Her overt sexuality and lack of diplomacy, combined with Henry VIII's decline into near madness, spelled her doom as the first connubial victim of Henry's executioner.

Although destined for a short but rich life as Queen of England, Anne's true legacy was the small ginger-haired toddler she left behind on her final trip to the Tower of London.

Elizabeth would grow to become one of the strongest and most well-remembered rulers of England, cautiously navigating a minefield of intruiges and plots, surviving her own time in the Tower of London with a political acumen that her mother sadly lacked.

A small ring bearing both Anne & Elizabeth's likeness inside, dated to the middle of Elizabeth's reign, may have been worn by the Queen herself (although this has not been verified).

**Portrait thought to be of Anne Boleyn, probably a later copy of an image from about 1534, c. 1536**

## PEMBROKE JACKET INFORMATION

| | |
|---|---|
| To Fit Bust | 30 (36, 42, 50, 58)"/ 76.5 (92, 107, 127.5, 148) cm |
| Finished Waist | 27 ¾ (33 ¾, 38, 45, 51)"/ 71 (86, 97, 115, 130) cm |
| Finished Bust | 33 (39, 45, 53, 61)"/ 84 (99.5, 115, 135, 155.5) cm |
| Skill Level | C 4 Advanced |
| Fiber A | Tilli Tomas, Milan (165yds /150m 1.75oz /50gr) Color A, Black 3 (4, 6, 8, 8, 10) balls |
| Fiber B, C, D | Tilli Tomas Beaded Milan Color B , Napolitan 1 (2, 2, 2, 2, 3) balls Color C , Dap. Grey 1 (2, 2, 2, 2, 3) balls Color D , Black 1 (2, 2, 2, 2, 3) balls |
| Beads | 22 (26, 30, 34, 34, 38) 12mm-Bronze Round Filigree Metal Beads 68 (76, 84, 92, 92, 100) 5mm Grey Freshwater pearls |
| Gauge | 18 sc x 24 rows = 4"/10cm worked in single crochet using size GUS/4mm. |
| Hook | Size GUS/4mm hook |
| Notions | Movable stitch markers or safety pins, darning needles, beading needle, 18 (19 1/2, 21, 22 1/2, 23 1/2) " / 46 (49.5, 53.5, 57.5, 60) cm separating zipper (or length to match finished piece, it's wisest to purchase this after garment is complete) black button thread, hook & eye (optional) |

## PEMBROKE JACKET STITCHES

- Sc – Single Crochet
- Dc – Double Crochet
- Hdc – Half Double Crochet
- B-Sc – Bead Single Crochet
- B-Hdc – Bead Half Double Crochet
- Sc2tog – Single Crochet 2 Together
- Dc2tog – Double Crochet 2 Together
- Sc3tog– Single Crochet 3 Together
- Dc3tog – Double Crochet 3 Together
- Flo – Front Loop Only
- Blo – Back Loop Only

## PEMBROKE JACKET TECHNIQUES

- PL – Picot Loop (7 Stitch)

*See Special Techniques, page 116, for full explanations on how to work the stitches and techniques listed above.*

## STRINGING THE BEADS

Yarns B, C & D are pre-beaded, the beads are strung on a separate strand of yarn which runs along the main yarn. The beads tend to show up better on the RS of the work when worked in a WS row, which is why I have designated certain rows to be worked in a specific direction. Yarn A is a smooth yarn and in two places in the pattern you are required to string larger beads onto A for specific bead placement.
Yarn A1 is the plain milano with 12m beads strung onto it and is used in Row 5 of the Yoke Chart.
Yarn A2 is the plain milano with 5m pearl beads strung onto it and is used in Row 13 of the Yoke Chart.
If the yarn is too thick to string the beads, they can also be strung on a separate string of button thread held along the working yarn.

## 6 ROUND/ROW TEXTURE PATTERN
Rounds 1-5: Ch1, sc all sts; sl st to join.
Round 6: Ch2, dc all sts; sl st to join.

## PEMBROKE JACKET
*Notes: The garment is worked from the neck down to the hem. Turn and ch1 at the beg of every row. Ch1 does NOT count as a sc. When following Chart, using guide arrows on the edge to note which direction to work.*

### NECKLINE
With C create picot foundation chain as foll: [Ch 7 sl st in 4th ch from hook] 32 (36, 40, 44, 48) times, end ch 3

Next Row: Turn work, ch 1, 1 sc into last ch from prev row, [1 sc into picot, 1 sc each next 2 ch] rep to end of row — 96 (108, 120, 132, 144) sts

### YOKE
Work charted pattern and increase 2 sts at each of the 4 corners every row as follows:

Row 1: Sc 12 (14, 16, 18, 20) sts, ch 3, sc 20 (22, 24, 26, 28) sts, ch 3, sc 32 (36, 40, 44, 48) sts, ch 3, sc 20 (22, 24, 26, 28) sts, ch 3, end sc 12 (14, 16, 18, 20) sts — 96 (108, 120, 132, 144) sts and 4 3-ch sps. spaces.
Row 2 (WS): [1 sc into each sc to ch sp, sc 3 into ch

**Detail: Beaded Crochet Neckline**

sp, mark center st of sc-3] four times, 1 sc each sc to end of row — 104 (116, 128, 140, 152) sts
Row 3 (RS): [1 sc into each sc to marked st, sc 3, marking center sc] four times, 1 sc each sc to end of row — 112 (124, 136, 148, 160) sts
Row 4 (RS): With A1, [1 hdc into each sc to marked st, hdc 3 marking center hdc] four times, 1 hdc each sc to end of row — 120 (132, 144, 156, 168) sts
Row 5 (WS): Hdc 16 (18, 20, 22, 24) sts [(hdc 2, b-hdc, hdc 3) rep to marked st, 3 hdc, mark center st], Hdc 28 (30, 32, 34, 36) sts [(hdc 2, b-hdc, hdc 3) rep to marked st, 3 hdc, mark center st], Hdc 40 (44, 48, 52, 56) sts [(hdc 2, b-hdc, hdc 3) rep to marked st, 3 hdc, mark center st], Hdc 28 (30, 32, 34, 36) sts [(hdc 2, b-hdc, hdc 3) rep to marked st, 3 hdc, mark center st], Hdc 16 (18, 20, 22, 24) sts [(hdc 2, b-hdc, hdc 3) rep to end — 128 (140, 152, 164, 176) sts
Row 6 (RS): [1 sc into each hdc to marker, sc 3, marking center st] four times, 1 sc each sc to end of row — 136 (148, 160, 172, 184) sts
Rows 7 (RS) & 8 (WS): With B, rep rows 2 & 3.
Rows 9 (RS) & 10 (WS): With D, rep rows 2 & 3 — 168 (180, 192, 204, 216) sts
Row 11 (RS): With C, sc 1 (ch 1, sk 1, sc 2) rep to marker, [sc 3, mark center st, (sc 2, ch 1, sk 1) rep to marker] three times, then rep once to end of row, end sc 1 — 176 (188, 200, 212, 224) sts
Row 12 (RS): With D, 1 sc into first st, [(3 sc into next 1-ch sp, sk 2 sc) rep to marker, sc 3, mark center st] four times, (3 sc into next 1-ch sp, sk 2 sc), rep to end of row — 184 (196, 208, 220, 232) sts
Row 13 (WS): With A2, work 1 b-sc into the center of each sc-3 group from Row 12 and into the center st at each corner. Sc all other sts, working 3 sc into each corner as in prev rounds.
Row 14 (RS): With A work 1 sc into each sc and b-sc, working 3 sc into each corner st as est.
Row 15 (RS): With B work 1 sc into each sc and b-sc, working 3 sc into each corner st as est.
Row 16 (WS): With B work 1 sc into each sc and b-sc, working 3 sc into each corner st as est.
Row 17 (WS): With D work 1 sc into each sc and b-sc, working 3 sc into each corner st as est.
Row 18 (RS): With C work 1 sc into each sc and b-sc, working 3 sc into each corner st as est.
Row 19 (RS): With D work 1 sc into each sc and b-sc, working 3 sc into each corner st as est – 248

(260, 272, 284, 296) sts

Rep Rows 16-19 until a total of 19 (20, 23, 26, 26) rows have been worked 248 (268, 304, 340, 352) sts – total in yoke. Break all colors and cont with A only (unbeaded).

## LEFT SLEEVE

Arrange piece so that the left shoulder edge of the yoke is facing you. Join A to left (back) corner of left shoulder edge and ch 8 (8, 12, 12, 12) sts

Join at front corner of left shoulder edge and sc 28 (30, 32, 34, 36) sts across left shoulder edge, then sc halfway across 8 (8, 12, 12, 12) sts chain. Place marker to note underarm point – 66 (70, 82, 90, 92) sts

Work in 6 Row Texture Patt and at the same time dec 1 st every round as foll:

Round 1: Sc 32 (34, 40, 44, 45) sts, mark the next st, sc to end of round.

Round 2: Work to 1 st before marked st, work 2 sts tog, move marker to this st, work to end of round — 65 (69, 81, 89, 91) sts

Working the decreases as sc2tog or dc2tog, depending on the round & keeping to the 6-row texture pattern, rep Round 2 until 51 (55, 58, 66, 68) sts rem.

Cont working even with no further decreasing, working 5 rounds of sc and 1 round of dc, until sleeve meas 8 (9, 10, 11, 12)"/20.5 (23, 25.5, 28, 30.5) cm from last row of yoke.

This is an excellent place to lengthen or shorten the sleeves as you desire.

### CUFF

*Note: Sl st to join and ch1 at beg of each rnd.*

Round 1 (RS): With B Sc around.
Rounds 2-4 (WS): Turn the work so the WS is facing, sc around.
Round 5 (WS): With D, sc around.
Round 6 (WS): With B, sc around.
Rep rounds 5 & 6 twice more.
Round 7 (WS): Rep Round 5.
Round 8 (WS): With C, sc around.
Rep Rounds 7 & 8 three times more.
Repeat for Right Sleeve, reversing shaping and working the cuff in the same manner as the Left.

## BODY

Turn and ch1 at the beg of every sc row, ch2 at beg of every dc row. Ch1 does NOT count as a sc, however ch2 DOES count as a dc.

Join A to the bottom front corner of the Left Front.

Row 1 (RS): Sc 31 (34, 39, 44, 46) sts across Left Front yoke, sc 8 (8, 12, 12, 12) sts along Left underarm, sc 70 (76, 86, 96, 100) sts across Back yoke, sc 8 (8, 12, 12, 12) sts along Right underarm, sc 31 (34, 39, 44, 46) sts along Right Front Yoke — 148 (160, 188, 208, 216) sts total.
Row 2 (WS): Sc to end of row.
Work in 6 row texture patt (used on sleeves) for 1 1/2 (1 3/4, 2, 2 1/4, 2 1/2)"/4 (4.5, 5, 5.5, 6.5) cm (or desired length) to start of bust decreasing. End with a WS row.

### BUST DECREASING

Cont in patt as est, work bust dec as follows, working dec as sc2tog, dc2tog, sc3tog & dc3tog depending on which row you're in:

Row 1: Work 37 (40, 47, 52, 54) sts, sc3tog, mark this st (Left Front dart). Then work 68 (74, 88, 98, 102) sts, sc3tog, mark this st (center back). Then work 37 (40, 47, 52, 54) sts, sc3tog, mark this st (Right Front dart), work to the end of the row – 142 (154, 182, 202, 210) sts.
Row 2 (WS): Work to 1 st before the first marker, work 3 sts tog, move marker up to this st. Work to next marker, work 2 sts tog, move marker up to this st, work to end — 139 (151, 179, 199, 207) sts.

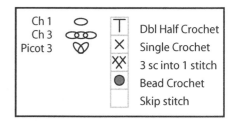

| | Ch 1 | ⬭ | T | Dbl Half Crochet |
| | Ch 3 | ⬭⬭⬭ | X | Single Crochet |
| | Picot 3 | ⬭ | XX | 3 sc into 1 stitch |
| | | | ● | Bead Crochet |
| | | | ☐ | Skip stitch |

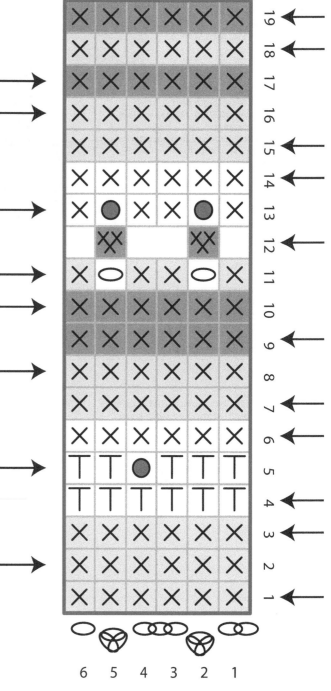

WHEN FOLLOWING THIS CHART, USE GUIDE ARROWS ON THE EDGES TO NOTE WHICH DIRECTION TO WORK.

Row 3 (RS): Work to 1 st before the first marker, work 3 sts tog, move marker up to this st. Work to next marker, work 2 sts tog, move marker up to this st, work to end — 136 (148, 176, 196, 204) sts.

Cont dec in this manner until 96 (105, 119, 133, 138) rem.

Work even in 6-Row Texture Patt with no further decreasing for 3 1/2 (3 3/4, 4, 4 1/4, 4 1/2)"/9 (9.5, 10, 11, 11.5) cm, or until work reaches natural waistline or desired length. End with a WS row.

## WAIST

Next Row: 1 hdc in each sc across work.

Next Row (WS): 1 hdc flo (wrong side loop) into each hdc.

Next Row (RS): 1 hdc blo (wrong side loop) into each hdc.

Rep last 2 rows twice, then work 1 more WS row.

## HIP SHAPING

Row 1 (RS): Join D and working all sts in sc, sc 5 (0, 0, 0, 5) sts, [sc 2 into next st, sc 6] rep to end of row — 109 (120, 136, 152, 157) sts

Rows 2, 4 & 6 (WS): Sc all sts.

Row 3: Next Row (RS): [Sc 7, sc 2 into next st] rep to last 5 (0, 0, 0, 5) sts, sc to end of row — 122 (135, 153, 171, 176) sts

Row 5 (RS): Sc 5 (0, 0, 0, 5) sts, [sc 2 into next st, sc 8] rep to end of row — 135 (150, 170, 190, 195) sts

## HEM BAND

*Note, in the Hem Band section, work on either Right or Wrong side of the work, however the yarn is currently situated.*

Row 1: With B, sc all sts

Rows 2-4: Sc all sts.

Row 5: With D, sc all sts.

Row 6: With B, sc all sts.

Rep rows 5 & 6 twice more.

Row 7: Rep Row 5.

Row 8: With C, sc all sts.

Rep Rows 7 & 8 twice more, then work work Row 7 once more.

## FINISHING

Weave in ends. Steam block piece, fold placket and collar band at rev st st row and stitch bound off edge to WS. Steam block hemmed collar and placket again.

Baste zipper into place on WS of placket fronts, hand or machine sew zipper to placket. Sew optional hook & eye at top placket edge to close jacket collar.

Annie Modesitt

PEMBROKE JACKET SCHEMATIC

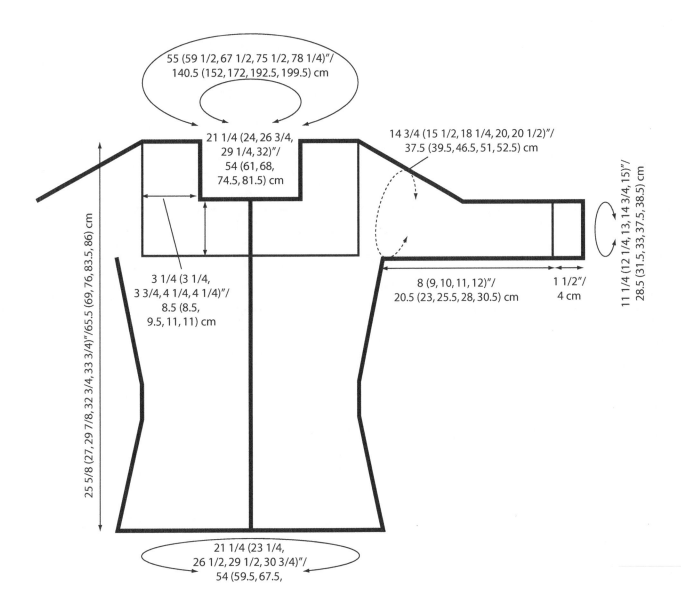

55 (59 1/2, 67 1/2, 75 1/2, 78 1/4)"/
140.5 (152, 172, 192.5, 199.5) cm

21 1/4 (24, 26 3/4,
29 1/4, 32)"/
54 (61, 68,
74.5, 81.5) cm

14 3/4 (15 1/2, 18 1/4, 20, 20 1/2)"/
37.5 (39.5, 46.5, 51, 52.5) cm

11 1/4 (12 1/4, 13, 14 3/4, 15)"/
28.5 (31.5, 33, 37.5, 38.5) cm

3 1/4 (3 1/4,
3 3/4, 4 1/4, 4 1/4)"/
8.5 (8.5,
9.5, 11, 11) cm

25 5/8 (27, 29 7/8, 32 3/4, 33 3/4)"/65.5 (69, 76, 83.5, 86) cm

8 (9, 10, 11, 12)"/
20.5 (23, 25.5, 28, 30.5) cm

1 1/2"/
4 cm

21 1/4 (23 1/4,
26 1/2, 29 1/2, 30 3/4)"/
54 (59.5, 67.5,

Pembroke Jacket 67

A comfortable, dressier alternative to the office cardigan, the Gloriana Jacket could be worn for day or dressed up for evening.
*Background: Canterbury Cathedral Interior*
*Gloriana Jacket modeled by Ellis Norris, knit by Annie Modesitt*

# Gloriana Jacket

The most powerful women of her time, Elizabeth I reigned a peaceful and prosperous realm for almost 45 years from 1558-1603.

No monarch can be universally loved, but "Good Queen Bess" came close.

A very popular figure to her subjects (to whom she considered herself "married"), Elizabeth I reigned for almost 45 years.

The child of Henry VIII and Anne Boleyn, Elizabeth was third in line to the throne at the time of Henry's death.

Accomplished and well educated, her youth was spent in turmoil as the political situation reversed when first her brother, Edward VI, then her sister, Mary I, ascended the throne and died.

Elizabeth behaved in ways contemporaries often considered "mannish" – riding, ruling and overwhelming her council with a strong – if at times indecisive – hand.

*Photo PKM*

**The Gripsholm Portrait**
(*though to be Elizabeth I of England*)
**c. 1563**

She sought to emulate the best political traits of her overpowering father, while at the same time reinforce her physical resemblance to "Good King Harry." (*Rumors of "bastardy birth" continued through her life*)

In this portrait, thought to be of *Gloriana* herself, Elizabeth appears in a rather masculine jacket and cap, which I've chosen to interpret as a cardigan "suit jacket."

## Gloriana Jacket Information

| | |
|---|---|
| To Fit Bust | 32 (36, 40, 44, 48, 53, 57)"/81.5 (92, 102, 112, 122.5, 135, 145.5) cm |
| Finished Bust | 36 (40, 44, 48, 52, 57, 61)"/92 (102, 112, 122.5, 132.5, 145.5, 155.5) cm |
| Total Length | 19¾ (21¼, 21½, 23¼, 23¼, 25, 25½)"/50.5 (54, 55, 59.5, 59.5, 64, 65) cm |
| Skill Level | K 5 Experienced |
| Fiber A | Artyarns, Silk Rhapsody (260yds/237m 3.5oz/100gr) #245 Raspberry Pink 4 (4, 5, 5, 6, 6, 7) skeins |
| Fiber B | Artyarns, Beaded Silk & Sequins (78yds/71m 1.75oz/50gr) #04 Setting Sun 2 (2, 2, 3, 3, 3, 4) skeins |
| Gauge | 16 sts x 24 rows = 4"/10cm in 7-stitch rib patt using needle size 7US/4.5mm |
| Needle | Size 7US/4.5mm |
| Notions | Darning needle, additional dpns or circ needles in smaller size for picking up sts (optional) 2"/5cm Belt Buckle (or desired size for your finished belt) |

## Gloriana Jacket Stitches

St st – Stockinette Stitch
Rev St st – Reverse St st
Sl st wyws – Slip st with yarn to the wrong side
Sl st wyrs – Slip st with yarn to the right side
K2tog-R – Knit 2 tog with a right slant
K2tog-L – Knit 2 tog with a left slant
YO – Yarn Over
GR Inc – Grandma Right Increase
GL Inc – Grandma Left Increase
GPR Inc – Grandma Purl Right Increase
GPL Inc – Grandma Purl Left Increase
VDD – Vertical Double Decrease

## Gloriana Jacket Techniques

5 St DKSS Edge – Double Knit Slip Stitch Edge
C4R – Cable 4 Right
C4L – Cable 4 Left
Reversible Cable
I-Cord Bind Off

*See Special Techniques, page 116, for full explanations on how to work the stitches and techniques listed above.*

## Gloriana Jacket Charts A1 & A2

Row 1 (RS): K1, wyrs sl1, k1, (DKSS edge) p2, sm, k1, [k1, p2, k1, sl 1, k1, p2, k1] 16 (18, 20, 22, 24, 26, 28) times, k1, sm, p2, k1, wyrs sl1, k1 (DKSS edge.)
Row 2 (WS): Sl 1 wyws, k1, sl 1 wyws, (DKSS edge), k2, sm, p1, [p1, k2, p3, k2, p1] 16 (18, 20, 22, 24, 26, 28) times, p1, sm, k2, sl 1 wyws, k1, sl 1 wyws (DKSS edge.)
Row 3: DKSS edge, p2, sm, GR Inc, k2, p2, VDD, [p2, k2, p2, k1, sl 1, k1] rep to last 12 sts, VDD, p2, k2, GL Inc, sm, p2, DKSS edge.
Row 4 (and all WS rows): Work in rib patt as est.
Row 5: DKSS edge, p2, sm, GR Inc, k3, p2, sl 1, p2, k2, p2, VDD, [p2, k2, p2, k1, sl 1, k1] rep to last 21 sts, VDD, p2, k2, p2, sl 1, p2, k3, GL Inc, p2, DKSS edge.
Row 7: Work to marker as est, inc 1 in st just past marker, k4, p2, [sl 1, p2, k2, p2] twice, VDD, [p2, k2, p2, k1, sl 1, k1] rep to last 30 sts, VDD, [p2, k2, p2, sl 1] twice, p2, k4, inc 1 in st before marker, sm, work to end in patt as est.
Row 9: Work to marker as est, inc 1 in st just past marker, p1, C4R, p2, [sl 1, p2, k2, p2] rep to next 3-st {k1, sl1, k1} group, VDD, [p2, k2, p2, k1, sl 1, k1] rep to last 3-st group, VDD, [p2, k2, p2, sl1], rep to 4 knit st group, C4L, k1, inc 1 in st before marker, sm, work to end in patt as est.
Row 9: Work to marker as est, inc 1 in st just past marker, p1, C4R, p2, [sl 1, p2, k2, p2] rep to next 3-st {k1, sl1, k1} group, VDD, [p2, k2, p2, k1, sl 1, k1] rep to last 3-st group, VDD, [p2, k2, p2, sl1], rep to 4 knit st group, C4L, p1, inc 1 in st before marker, sm, work to end in patt as est.
Note: When all 3-st sections {k1, sl 1, k1} have been dec as VDD, work across back with no further decreasing, slipping VDDs from prev rows.
Row 11: Work to marker as est, inc 1 in st just past marker, p2, k4, p2, [sl 1, p2, k2, p2] rep to next 3-st {k1, sl1, k1} group, VDD, [p2, k2, p2, k1, sl 1, k1] rep to last 3-st group, VDD, [p2, k2, p2, sl1], rep to 4 knit st group, k4, p2, inc 1 in st before marker, sm, work to end in patt as est.
Row 13: Work to marker as est, inc 1 in st just past marker, k1, p2, C4R, p2, [sl 1, p2, k2, p2] rep to next 3-st {k1, sl1, k1} group, VDD, [p2, k2, p2, k1, sl 1, k1] rep to last 3-st group, VDD, [p2, k2, p2, sl1], rep to 4 knit st group, C4L, p2, k1, inc 1 in st before marker, sm, work to end in patt as est.
Row 15: Work to marker as est, inc 1 in st just past marker, k2, p2, k4, p2, [sl 1, p2, k2, p2] rep to next 3-st {k1, sl1, k1} group, VDD, [p2, k2, p2, k1, sl 1, k1] rep to last 3-st group, VDD, [p2, k2, p2, sl1], rep to 4 knit st group, k4, p2, k2, inc 1 in st before marker, sm, work to end in patt as est.
Row 17: Work to marker as est, inc 1 in st just past marker, k3, p2, C4R, p2, [sl 1, p2, k2, p2] rep to next 3-st {k1, sl1, k1} group, VDD, [p2, k2, p2, k1, sl 1, k1] rep to last 3-st group, VDD, [p2, k2, p2, sl1], rep to 4 knit st group, C4L, p2, k3, inc 1 in st before marker, sm, work to end in patt as est.
Row 19: Work to marker as est, inc 1 in st just past marker, k4, p2, k4, p2, [sl 1, p2, k2, p2] rep to next 3-st {k1, sl1, k1} group, VDD, [p2, k2, p2, k1, sl 1, k1] rep to last 3-st group, VDD, [p2, k2, p2, sl1], rep to 4 knit st group, k4, p2, k4, inc 1 in st before marker, sm, work to end in patt as est.
Row 21: Work to marker as est, inc 1 in st just past marker, C4R, p2, C4R, p2, [sl 1, p2, k2, p2] rep to next 3-st {k1, sl1, k1} group, VDD, [p2, k2, p2, k1, sl 1, k1] rep to last 3-st group, VDD, [p2, k2, p2, sl1], rep to 4 knit st group, C4L, p2, C4L, k1 inc 1 in st before marker, sm, work to end in patt as est.

(written instructions are not given for this chart after Row 22, or for Charts B1 and B2)

### Gloriana Jacket Back Shaping

# GLORIANA JACKET

## BODY

### HEM

With A and using a long tail cast on, CO 156 (174, 192, 210, 228, 246, 264) sts

Setup (WS): Establish rib patt as foll: Sl 1 wyws, k1, Sl 1 wyws, k2, (5 st DKSS edge), pm, p1, [p1, k2, p3, k2, p1] 16 (18, 20, 22, 24, 26, 28) times, p1, pm, k2, Sl 1 wyws, k1, Sl 1 wyws (5 st DKSS edge.)

Working from written instructions or following Charts A1 Right & A2 Left as you prefer, establish patt as foll:

Work Rows 1 & 2 of Charts A1 Right & A2 Left until work meas 3¼ (3½, 3½, 3¾, 3½, 3¾, 3 ¾)"/8.5 (9, 9, 9.5, 9, 9.5, 9.5) cm from CO. *Chart Note: Non charted sts in middle of rows are worked in patt as est.*

In last row add 2 stitch markers 42 (51, 51, 60, 60, 69, 69) sts in from each edge to mark the underarm points. Back sts = 72 (72, 90, 90, 108, 108, 126) sts between markers.

### WAIST & LOWER LAPEL SHAPING

*(Cont in Charts A1 Right & A2 Left)*
*Construction Note: In this section the waist shaping is created by converting each 9-st rib motif into a 7-st rib motif. The lapels are created by increasing 1 st at each lapel every RS row, worked 6 sts in from each edge. In the chart the new lapel stitches are shown in light pink.*

Working from written instructions or following charts as you prefer, establish waist and lapel shaping to Row 22, which adds 2 sts (1 st each lapel edge) every RS row and incorporates those sts into the charted lapel cable motif, and converts the 9-st rib motifs into 7-st rib motifs as shown in the chart.

*Note: At Row 38 of Charts A1 Left & A1 Right, cables begin to be worked on the WRONG side of work as well as the RS:*

**Gloriana Neck Shaping**

Row 38 (WS): Sl 1 wyws, k1, Sl 1 wyws, k2, [C4L, p2] twice, work in rib as est to last 17 sts, [p2, c4R] twice, k2, Sl 1 wyws, k1, Sl 1 wyws.
Work Charts A1 Right & A2 Left through Row 42 of Charts A, then continue working in Charts B1 Right & B2 Left with no further lapel increasing until piece meas 13 (14, 14, 15, 15, 16, 16)"/33.5 (36, 36, 38.5, 38.5, 41, 41) cm from cast on, end with a WS row.

AT THE SAME TIME Cont working decreases across back until all 9-st rib motifs have been converted to 7-st rib motifs — 164 (178, 192, 206, 220, 234, 248) sts total.

### DIVIDE FOR ARMHOLES

Working Charts C1 Right & C2 Left, divide work as follows:

Row 1 (RS): K1, sl 1 wyrs, k1, p2 [k2, p4] twice, [k4, p2] twice, [sl 1, p2, k2, p2] rep to last 29 sts, [p2, k4] twice, [p4, k2] twice, p2, k1, sl 1 wyrs, k1.

Row 2 (WS): Sl 1 wyws, k1, Sl 1 wyws, k2, [p2, k4] twice, [p4, k2] twice, [p1, k2, p2, k2] rep until 54 (61, 61, 68, 68, 75, 75) sts have been worked, you should be at side marker. Slip next 56 (56, 70, 70, 84, 84, 98) Back sts onto holder to work later. Resuming with rem 54 (61, 61, 68, 68, 75, 75) sts, join a second ball of yarn and work in rib patt as est to last 29 sts, [k2, p4] twice, [k4, p2] twice, k2, Sl 1 wyws, k1, Sl 1 wyws.

### BEG UPPER LAPEL SHAPING

*(Cont in Charts C1 Right & C2 Left)*

Construction Note: The YO in Row 3 is the point of lapel fold, generating from this YO will be a column of slipped sts creating the lapel fold line. All future lapel increases will be worked to the outside of this initial YO, the new sts created will be worked in seed st to create a nicely curving fabric. You will be working both Fronts at the same time in the following section.

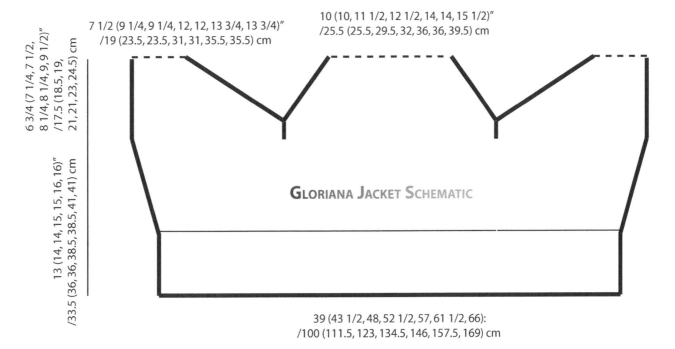

7 1/2 (9 1/4, 9 1/4, 12, 12, 13 3/4, 13 3/4)" /19 (23.5, 23.5, 31, 31, 35.5, 35.5) cm

10 (10, 11 1/2, 12 1/2, 14, 14, 15 1/2)" /25.5 (25.5, 29.5, 32, 36, 36, 39.5) cm

6 3/4 (7 1/4, 7 1/2, 8 1/4, 8 1/4, 9, 9 1/2)" /17.5 (18.5, 19, 21, 21, 23, 24.5) cm

13 (14, 14, 15, 15, 16, 16)" /33.5 (36, 36, 38.5, 38.5, 41, 41) cm

**GLORIANA JACKET SCHEMATIC**

39 (43 1/2, 48, 52 1/2, 57, 61 1/2, 66): /100 (111.5, 123, 134.5, 146, 157.5, 169) cm

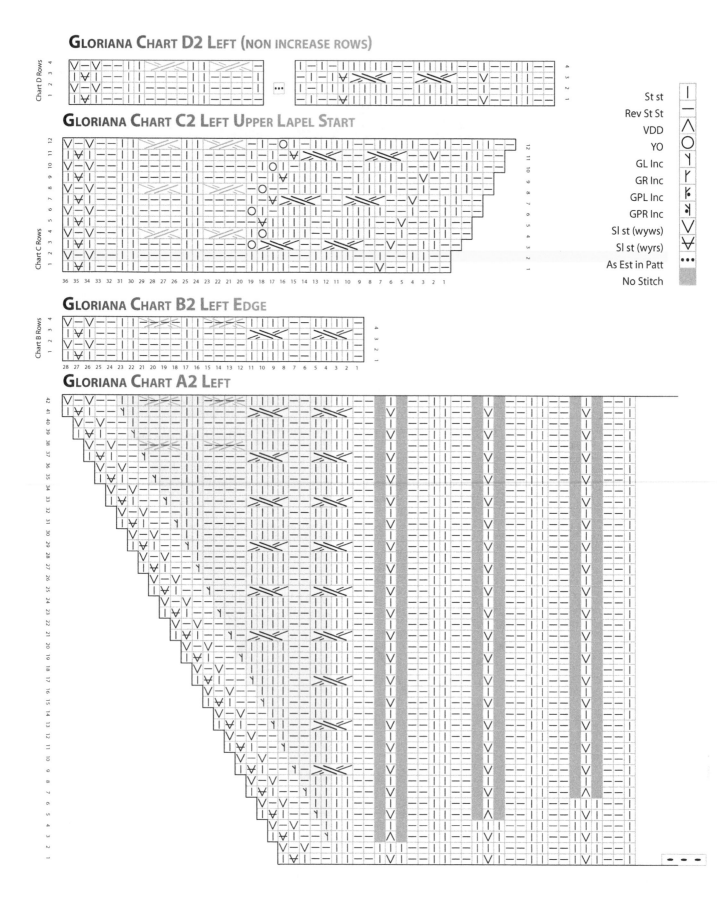

### Gloriana Chart D2 Left (non increase rows)

### Gloriana Chart C2 Left Upper Lapel Start

### Gloriana Chart B2 Left Edge

### Gloriana Chart A2 Left

St st
Rev St St
VDD
YO
GL Inc
GR Inc
GPL Inc
GPR Inc
Sl st (wyws)
Sl st (wyrs)
As Est in Patt
No Stitch

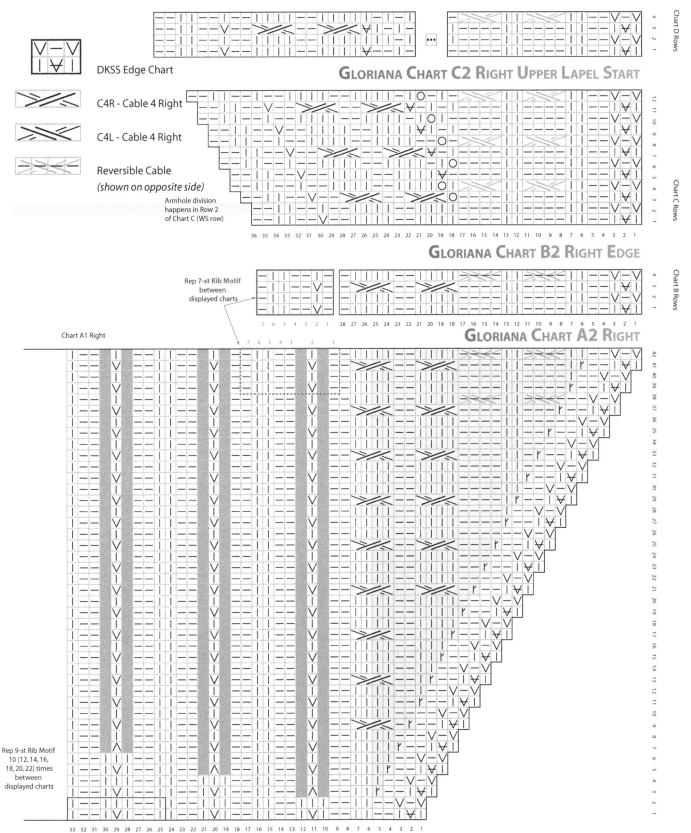

GLORIANA CHART D2 RIGHT (NON INCREASE ROWS)

DKSS Edge Chart

C4R - Cable 4 Right

C4L - Cable 4 Right

Reversible Cable
*(shown on opposite side)*

GLORIANA CHART C2 RIGHT UPPER LAPEL START

Armhole division
happens in Row 2
of Chart C (WS row)

GLORIANA CHART B2 RIGHT EDGE

Rep 7-st Rib Motif
between
displayed charts

Chart A1 Right

GLORIANA CHART A2 RIGHT

Rep 9-st Rib Motif
10 (12, 14, 16,
18, 20, 22) times
between
displayed charts

*An accomplished needlewoman, the 11-year old Elizabeth embroidered the cover to her translation of The Miroir or Glasse of the Synneful Soul as a gift for her step mother, Katherine Parr, the 6th wife of Henry VIII.*

Row 3 (RS): RIGHT FRONT: K1, sl 1 wyrs, k1, p2, [k2, p4] twice, YO, [C4R, p2] twice, [sl 1, p2, k2, p2] rep to end of Right Front sts. Following Chart C2 Left, reverse shaping for LEFT FRONT (rem sts), working both Fronts at the same time.

Row 4 (WS): LEFT FRONT: Sl 1 wyws, k1, Sl 1 wyws, k2, [p2, C4L] twice, p1, YO, [p4, k2] twice, [p1, k2, p2, k2] rep to end of Left Front sts.

Photo PKM

Following chart B1 Right, reverse shaping for RIGHT FRONT (rem sts.)

Cont in Charts C1 Right & C2 Left as est until 8 (8, 8, 12, 12, 12, 12) sts have been increased in the upper lapel, working newly increased sts in a double seed st patt as est.

Cont with no further increasing (see Charts D1 Right & D2 Left for visual assistance) until piece meas 6¾ (7¼, 7½, 8¼, 8¼, 9, 9½)"/17.5 (18.5, 19, 21, 21, 23, 24.5) cm from armhole divide.

AND AT THE SAME TIME when work meas 1 (1½, 1¾, 2½, 2½, 3¼, 3¾)"/2.5 (4, 4.5, 6.5, 6.5, 8.5, 9.5) cm from armhole divide, begin shaping shoulder as foll:

Mark the 18th st in from each armhole edge *(it should be a slip st, if not mark the nearest sl st)*

This will be the dec point of the shoulder shaping *(this is not shown on the chart.)*

While working lap inc as est, work a VDD at this shoulder dec point stitch in every RS row 16 times (total dec of 32 sts) — 30 (37, 37, 48, 48, 55, 55) sts rem in each Front. Slip rem sts on holder to work later.

## UPPER BACK

Slip 56 (56, 70, 70) sts from holder onto needle and work in rib patt as est until back meas 1 (1½, 1¾, 2½, 2½, 3¼, 3¾)"/2.5 (4, 4.5, 6.5, 6.5, 8.5, 9.5) cm from armhole divide, ending with a WS row. Begin shaping shoulder as foll:

Next Row (RS): Work in patt as est for 16 sts, K2tog-R, work in rib as est until 18 sts rem, k2tog-L, work to end.
Next Row (WS): Work in rib patt as est, purling dec sts from prev row.
Work last 2 rows a total of 8 (8, 12, 10, 14, 14, 18) times — 40 (40, 46, 50, 56,

56, 62) sts rem. Work even until Back meas same as Fronts at Armhole edge.

## JOIN SHOULDERS

Slip 8 (8, 8, 10, 12, 16, 16) sts from Right Front Armhole Edge onto needle and align with Right Back Armhole Edge so Right Side of garment is together (wrong sides facing out.) Leave rem 22 (29, 29, 38, 36, 39, 39) Front sts on holder. Join Right shoulder using a 3 needle bind off, rep for Left shoulder. 24 (24, 30, 30, 32, 24, 30) sts rem at Back Neck. Break Yarn A.

## COLLAR

Slip 22 (29, 29, 38, 36, 39, 39) Right Front Lapel sts, PU 2 sts at join point, slip 24 (24, 30, 30, 32, 24, 30) Back sts, PU 2 sts at join point, slip 22 (29, 29, 38, 36, 39, 39) Left Front lapel sts onto needle – 72 (86, 92, 110, 108, 106, 112) sts total. Turn work

*Construction Note: At this point the WS of jacket (but RS of Lapel) will be facing you, you will be ready to start at the Left Front Lapel edge. From this point on the side facing you will be called the Right Side, note that the orientation of the DKSS edges will not change.*

Row 1 (RS): With Yarn B, k18 (25, 25, 32, 28, 27, 27) sts, VDD, k15 (15, 18, 20, 23, 23, 26) sts, k2tog-R, k15 (15, 18, 20, 23, 23, 26) sts, VDD, K18 (25, 25, 32, 28, 27, 27) sts – 69 (83, 89, 107, 105, 103, 109) sts
Row 2 (WS): P17 (24, 24, 31, 27, 26, 26) sts, [p1, k1] 15 (15, 18, 20, 23, 23, 26) times, p2tog, turn work.
Row 3 (RS): There are now 47 (54, 60, 71, 73, 72, 78) sts on the LH needle and 17 (24, 24, 31, 27, 26, 26) sts on the RH needle. Sl 1, K29 (29, 35, 39, 45, 45, 51) sts, k2tog-L, turn work.
Row 4 (WS): Sl 1, [k1, p1] rep to slipped

**Gloriana Jacket Collar and Sleeve Detail**

st from prev row, p slipped st tog with next lapel st (dec of 1 st), turn work.

Row 5 (RS): Sl 1, knit to slipped st from prev row, k slipped st tog with next lapel st (dec of 1 st)

Rep Rows 4 and 5 rows once more, 14 (21, 21, 28, 24, 23, 23) sts in each lapel yet to be decreased. End with a RS row.

## SHORT ROW SHAPING

Row 1 (WS): Sl 1, [k1, p1] rep to slipped st from prev row, [k1, p1] twice, W&T.

Row 2 (RS): Knit to slipped st from prev row, k slipped st, k3, W&T.

Row 3 (WS): Sl 1, [k1, p1] rep to wrapped st from prev row, [k1, p1] twice, (W&T.)

Row 4 (RS): Knit to wrapped st from prev row, k wrapped st (moving wrap up onto needle and working along with stitch), k3, W&T.

Rep last 2 rows 1 (3, 3, 5, 4, 4, 4) times, (6 (5, 5, 4, 4, 3, 3) sts rem unworked in each lapel.) Then work one more RS row to the end, working DKSS edge as est.

Next Row (WS): Work DKSS edge as est, work in [p1, k1] patt as est to last 3 sts, work DKSS edge.

Next Row (RS): Work DKSS edge as est, knit to last 3 sts, work DKSS edge.

Rep last 2 rows twice more (6 full non-short rows), end with a RS row.

Next Row (WS): Work DKSS edge as est, knit to last 3 sts, work DKSS edge.

## I-CORD BIND OFF

Preparation (RS Row): K1, insert Right needle into next 2 sts on LH needle AS IF knitting 2 tog-R and slip them to RH needle. Rotate RH needle and slip these 2 sts back onto LH needle so their placement is reversed. Knit these 2 sts. Slip 3 sts just worked from RH needle back onto LH needle and knit them again. Slip these 3 sts back to LH needle. Work an I-cord BO across all collar sts, tie off last st.

## SLEEVE

With A, pick up and knit 77 (91, 91, 98, 98, 105, 119) sts, around armhole.

## SHORT ROW BAND

Starting at bottom of armhole set up sleeve sts as foll:

Row 1 (RS): [K1, p2, sl1, p2, k1] 11 (13, 13, 14, 14, 15, 17) times, turn work.

Row 2 (WS): [P1, k2, p1, k2, p1], cont in patt as est to last 3 sts, W&T.

Row 3 (RS): [Sl 1, p2, k2, p2], cont in patt as est to last 3 sts, W&T.

Next Row: Cont in rib as est across row to 7 sts before last wrapped st, W&T.

Rep last row 8 times more, working 7 fewer sts in each row, ending with a WS row.

Next Row (RS): Work to end of row in rib as est, slipping wraps up onto needle and working along with each wrapped st.

Next Row (WS): Work in rib as est, dealing with wrapped sts as in prev row.

Contrast Band (6 rounds total)

Next Round: With B, knit around all sts.

Next Round: With A, [k1, sl 1] rep to end of round.

Rep last 2 rounds once more, then with B knit 1 round.

Next Round: With A knit all sts.

Work Short Row Band & Contrast Band twice more (6 bands total), then with B only, work an I-cord bind off as directed in Special Techniques section.

## BELT

CO 23 sts.

Row 1 (RS): K1, sl 1 wyrs, k1 (DKSS edge), k17, k1, sl 1 wyrs, k1.

Row 2 (WS): Sl 1 wyws, k1, Sl 1 wyws, [k1, p1] rep to last 3 sts, Sl 1 wyws, k1, Sl 1 wyws.

Rep last two rows until belt meas finished waist + 8"/20cm, or desired length. End with a WS row.

## BELT TIP

Row 1 (RS): Work DKSS edge, k15, W&T.

Row 2 (and all WS rows): [k1, p1] rep to last 3 sts, work DKSS edge as est.

Row 3 (RS): Work DKSS edge, k to 2 sts before last W&T, W&T.

Rep last 2 rows until no non DKSS sts rem to be worked, end with a WS row.

Next Row (RS): Work an I-Cord bind off as directed in Special Techniques section.

Secure cast on end of belt around the center bar of 2"/5cm belt buckle (there will be some gathering of fabric) and stitch in place.

### GlorianaJacketBeltDetail

The slightest bit of fullness in the hips and upper thighs of the straight Falkland Skirt make it walkable, wearable, and very flattering.

*Background: Falkland Castle Interior*

*Falkland Skirt modeled by Ellis Norris, knit by Annie Modesitt*

# Falkland Skirt

Both the son and father of beheaded monarchs, James VI of Scotland and First of England occupied a singular place in history.

The only child of Mary, Queen of Scots (who was beheaded at the order of Elizabeth I), the orphaned James was raised by his Calvinist uncles and advisors to rule Scotland and England.

James styled himself "King of Great Britain and Ireland" and took the Protestant princess Anne of Denmark as his queen.

The battles with Parliament over his Jacobean court's profligate spending set the tone for his son, Charles II's, disdain of the same governing body during his own reign.

James also passed on his love for expensive and questionable companionship to his son.

Charles' contempt for Parliament would set in motion the actions that led to a long civil war, culminating in his beheading in front of Inigo Jones' Banqueting House which, in sad irony, was commissioned by James.

Photo The National Portrait Gallery, London

**James VI of Scotland at 8 Years by Rowland Lockey (attributed) after A. Bronckorst, c. 1574**

In the painting of James at age eight, he is shown in a rich but fittingly modest outfit of white padded doublet with ridged sleeves and a small ruff. His full green velvet breeches were the inspiration for my simple, regal skirt.

## FALKLAND SKIRT INFORMATION

| | |
|---|---|
| To fit Hip | 28 (33, 38, 43, 48, 53, 58)"/71.5 (84, 97. 109.5, 122.5, 135, 148) cm |
| Finished Hip | 38 (43, 48, 53, 58, 63, 68)"/97 (109.5, 122.5, 135, 148, 160.5, 173.5) cm |
| Total Length | 26 (28, 30, 32, 34, 36, 38")/66.5 (71.5, 76.5, 81.5, 86.5 92, 97) cm |
| Skill Level | K 2 Easy |
| Fiber | Trendsetter, Bombay (ribbon) (120yds/109m 1.75oz/50gr) Olive 506, 6 (7, 7, 8, 9, 10, 10) balls |
| Gauge | 16 sts x 23 rows = 4"/10cm in St st using size 9US/5.5mm needle. |
| Needles | 9US/5.5mm (add'l size: 8US/6mm) 36" circular needle. |
| Notions | 25 (28, 31, 33, 36, 39, 42)"/64 (71, 78, 85, 92, 99, 106) cm 1" elastic |

## FALKLAND SKIRT STITCHES

St st – Stockinette Stitch
Rev St st — Reverse St st
K2tog-L – Knit 2 tog with a left slant
VDD – Vertical Double Decrease

*See Special Techniques, page 116, for full explanations on how to work the stitches and techniques listed above.*

## FALKLAND SKIRT CHART TEXT

Round 1: [P1, k2, p1] five times.
Rounds 2-6: Rep Round 1.
Round 7: P1, k2, p2, k10, p2, k2, p1.
Rounds 8-18: Rep Round 7.
Round 19: P1, k2, p1, k12, p1, k2, p1.
Rounds 20-22: Rep round 19.
Round 23: P1, k18, p1.
Round 24: P1, k8, k2tog-L, k8, p1.
Round 25: P1, k17, p1.
Round 26: P1, k7, VDD, k7, p1.
Round 27: P1, k15, p1.
Round 28: P1, k6, VDD, k6, p1.
Round 29: P1, k13, p1.
Round 30: P1, k5, VDD, k5, p1.
Round 31: P1, k11, p1.
Round 32: P1, k4, VDD, k4, p1.
Round 33: P1, k9, p1.

# FALKLAND SKIRT

*Notes: To make a longer skirt, work round 23 until skirt is desired length. For a larger waist, do not work all 5 decrease rounds. Stop at desired waist meas and move on to waistband.*

## HEM

With smaller circular needles cast on 160 (180, 200, 220, 240, 260, 280) sts. Work Skirt Chart, working pattern repeat 8 (9, 10, 11, 12, 13, 14) times around.

Continue as est until Round 6 is complete.

Change to larger needles and continue as est until Round 23 is complete. Rep Round 23 until skirt meas 22 (24, 26, 28, 30, 32, 34)"/56 (61, 66.5, 71.5, 76.5, 81.5, 86.5) cm or desired length from hem *(skirt should be 2"/5 cm below natural waistline).*

Work chart Rounds 24-33 – 88 (99, 110, 121, 132, 143, 154) sts.

## WAISTBAND

Rep Round 33 for 2"/5cm more.

Turning Ridge: Purl all sts.

## WAISTBAND FACING

Switch to smaller needles and work in St st for 2"/5cm. Bind off all stitches with larger needle.

## FINISHING

Steam block piece. Turn waistband over at turning ridge and stitch bound off end to wrong side of work, leaving a 1"/2.5cm opening.

Measure a piece of elastic to fit natural waistline (non stretched) plus 2"/5cm. Pin one end of elastic to wrong side of skirt to anchor it, thread opposite end around the waistband, entering and exiting at 1"/2.5cm hole.

*Tip: Pin a large safety pin to the end of the elastic to aid in threading through the waistband.*

Sew waistband opening closed. Weave in ends.

## FALKLAND SKIRT SCHEMATIC

22 (24 3/4, 27 1/2, 30 1/4, 33, 35 3/4, 38 1/2)"/ 56 (63, 70, 77, 84, 91, 98) cm

22 (24, 26, 28, 30, 32, 34)"/56 (61, 66.5, 71.5, 76.5, 81.5, 86.5) cm

38 (43, 48, 53, 58, 63, 68)"/ 97 (109.5, 122.5, 135, 148, 160.5, 173.5) cm

| | |
|---|---|
| St st | I |
| Rev St St | — |
| K2tog-L | ◺ |
| VDD | ∧ |

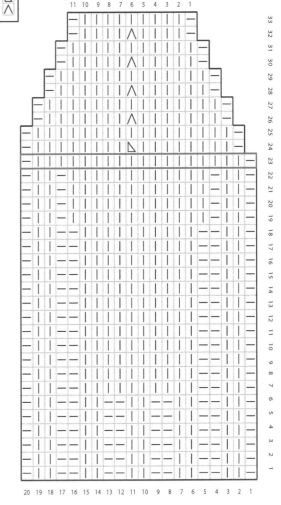

Garment & Background Photo: Annie Modesitt

**A warm hat which is also a fun and challenging project is a delight for both the knitter and the recipient.**

*Background: Canterbury Interior*

*Admiral Anja Hat modeled by Kristen Klemmen, knit by Annie Modesitt*

# Admiral Anja Hat

A simple colorwork hat with decorative earflaps, this would be a great gift piece for both men and women.

Charles Howard was a survivor and a victor.

He neatly ties together the other characters in our English Renaissance section, having been a cousin to Anne Boleyn and Elizabeth Tudor (his father, William, was Anne's mother's half brother) and commissioner and ambassador under James I.

While it is not certain that this image is *actually* of Charles himself, I like to think it *is* him, home from a long voyage, warming his tired body by the fire and wearing his favorite cap and full collar.

Charles' lifelong connection with the sea began in youth when he served under his father, the Lord Admiral, and continued throughout his career.

**Unknown man**
*(formerly thought to be Charles Howard, 1st Earl of Nottingham)*
**c. 1625**

Named Lord High Admiral himself in 1585, Charles was chiefly responsible for the English victory over the Spanish Armada.

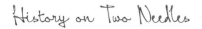

## ADMIRAL ANJA HAT INFORMATION

| | |
|---|---|
| Head Circ | 16 (20, 24)"/41 (51, 61) cm. |
| Skill Level | K 3 Intermediate |
| Fiber | Trendsetter, Merino 6 |
| | (136yds/124m 1.75oz/50gr) per skein |
| | Color A, 100 White, 2 balls |
| | Color B, 2029 Wine, 2 balls |
| Gauge | 24 sts x 30 rows = 4"/10cm |
| | in St st (colorwork) using |
| | needle size 5 US/3.75mm. |
| Needles | 5 US/3.75mm (24" circular and dpns) |
| Notions | Darning needle |

## ADMIRAL ANJA HAT STITCHES

St st – Stockinette Stitch
Rev St st – Reverse St st
Sl st wyws – Slip st with yarn to the wrong side
Sl st wyrs – Slip st with yarn to the right side
K2tog-L – Knit 2 tog with a left slant
VDD – Vertical Double Decrease
GR Inc – Grandma Right Increase

## ADMIRAL ANJA HAT TECHNIQUES

DKSS Edge – Double Knit Slip Stitch Edge
Twisted Cord

*See Special Techniques, page 116, for full explanations on how to work the stitches and techniques listed above.*

## ADMIRAL'S HAT

### HAT BOTTOM
With A, CO 88 (110, 132) sts onto circular needle. Join work, place marker to note start of round. Knit 7 rounds, purl 1 round to create a facing turning ridge.

Next round: [K 11, GR inc] 8 (10, 12) times — 96 (120, 144) sts. Knit 8 rounds in St st.

### BEGIN CHARTED PATT
Join B and work Row 1 of charted patt 4 (5, 6) times around work, then cont working in patt as est to row 58 of chart. As circumference of hat gets smaller, you will need to change to DPNs or the magic loop method on a larger circular needle.

Break yarn, leaving an 8"/40cm tail. Draw tail through rem 8 (10, 12) sts, weave in end. Steam block piece. Turn facing up at turning ridge and stitch to WS of work.

### EAR FLAPS
*Note: Only the smallest size ear flap is charted, use the chart and written instructions as a reference point for the larger sizes.*

Choose the best looking section of the hat and mark this point at the bottom edge with a safety pin as the FRONT.

Count back 12 (16, 20) sts from center point of the front (centered in a motif), Insert a dpn into the next 23 (27, 31) sts along turning ridge, picking them up, but not knitting them at this time.

With RS facing, join a strand of A and begin working earflap as foll:

Row 1 (RS): DKSS edge, p2, k to last 5 sts, p2, DKSS edge.
Row 2 (WS): DKSS edge, k2, [p1, k1] rep to last 5 sts, k2, DKSS edge.

Row 3 (RS): DKSS edge, p2, k6 (8, 10), sl 1, k6 (8, 10), p2, DKSS edge.
Rep last 2 rows 3 (4, 5) more times, then work 1 more WS row.

### BEG DEC
Next Row (RS): Work as est to 1 st before slipped st, VDD, work as est to end of row.
Next Row (WS): Work in patt as est, purl VDD from prev row.
Rep last 2 rows until 3 sts rem. End with a VDD. Tie off last st. Repeat for opposite ear flap.

### TIES
Using either or both colors of yarn (color B was used in the sample), create a twisted cord (see Special Techniques, page 116, to the desired length and stitch in place at the end of the earflap.

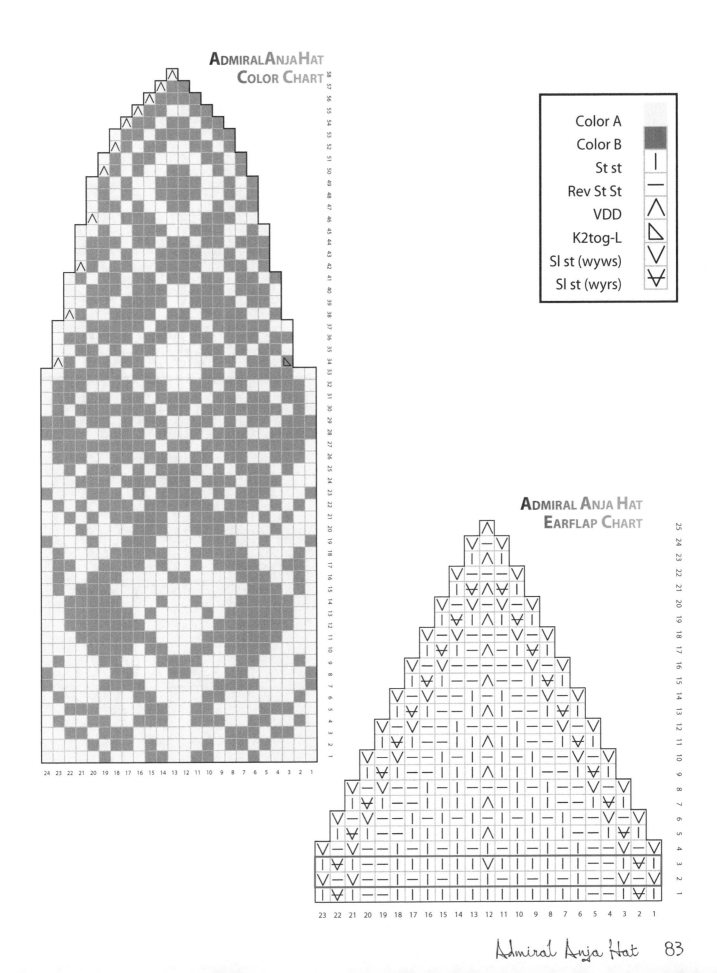

Annie Modesitt

**ADMIRAL ANJA HAT
COLOR CHART**

**ADMIRAL ANJA HAT
EARFLAP CHART**

| | |
|---|---|
| Color A | |
| Color B | |
| St st | |
| Rev St St | |
| VDD | |
| K2tog-L | |
| Sl st (wyws) | |
| Sl st (wyrs) | |

Deceptively easy to knit with the Cha Cha, the Nottingham Hoyle Ruff is given a firm structure with merino ribbing.

*Background: Canterbury Cathedral Interior*
*Nottingham Hoyle Ruff modeled by Kristen Klemmen, knit by Annie Modesitt*

*Garment & Background Photo: Annie Modesitt*

# Nottingham Hoyle Ruff

*The architecture of an Elizabethan ruff as it softens into a Stuart collar is determined by the firmness of the fabric.*

I love collars.

This striking collar acts as a structured scarf, and can enhance and add elegance to a mundane winter coat.

The soft ruffles are built onto a merino "body," which is shaped with short rows to sit gracefully around the shoulders.

The ruffles themselves are created using a novelty yarn, Cha Cha by Trendsetter, and worked in simple stockinette stitch.

Oversized ruffs (ruffled collars) became–unexpectedly–a status symbol throughout the reign of Queen Elizabeth I and into the reign of James VI, when they began to soften and flatten, eventually layering into the squared, soft, lace collars of the Stuart era.

In the late 1600s some collars evolved to suit the religious views of the Puritans in the simple, iconic "Pilgrim Collar," which almost every American child has worn in an elementary school pageant.

*Photo The National Portrait Gallery, London*

**Unknown man** *(formerly thought to be Charles Howard, 1st Earl of Nottingham)*
**c. 1625**

| N-H Ruff Pattern Info | |
|---|---|
| Finished Meas | 36"/92cm long by 6½"/17cm at widest point. |
| Skill Level | K 3 Intermediate |
| Fiber A | Trendsetter, Cha Cha Novelty ribbon yarn (72yds/66m 3.5oz/100gr) Ecru, 1 ball |
| Fiber B | Trendsetter, Merino 6 (136yds/124m 1.75oz/50gr White, 1 ball |
| Notions | Waste yarn for cast on, darning needle, 1"/2.5cm inch button |
| Gauge | 22 sts x 32 rows = 4"/10cm in St st in B using needle size 6US/4mm. |
| Needle | Size 6US/4mm 36" circ needle (plus add'l circ needle in same size, any length.) |

| N-H Ruff Stitches |
|---|
| St st – Stockinette Stitch |
| Rev St st — Reverse St st |
| W&T – Wrap & Turn |

| N-H Ruff Techniques |
|---|
| Cha Cha Ruffle |

*See Special Techniques, page 116, for full explanations on how to work the stitches and techniques listed above.*

# NOTTINGHAM HOYLE RUFF

## CAST ON

Using any provisional cast on method (see Special Techniques, page 116, CO 144

Next row (RS): With A, Knit.
Next row (WS): Knit.

## BEGIN SHAPING

Next row (RS): K12, p1, (k2, p2) rep until 12 sts rem, W&T.
Next row (WS): Work in rib as est until 12 sts rem, W&T.
Next row (RS): Work in rib as est until 12 sts before last W&T (108 sts worked), W&T.
Next row (WS): Work in rib as est until 12 sts before last W&T (96 sts worked), W&T.
Cont as est until only 12 sts rem to be worked before next W&T.

You should be in the center of the work, on a RS row. Work in rib as est to the last 13 sts, slipping wraps onto needle and working together with wrapped sts, p1, k12.

Next row (WS): K13, work in rib as est to last 13 sts, slipping wraps onto needle and working together with wrapped sts, k13.

## BUTTONHOLE

Next row (RS): K2, sl 1, BO 3, k to end of row.
Next row (WS): Knit to bound off sts, CO 3 sts, k3.

## ADD CENTER RUFFLE

Next row (RS): Cont with A, k72, keep yarn to WS of work. Join B, and working as described in the special techniques section, purl 60 (12 sts rem). Turn work.
Next row (WS): Cont with B, knit 120 sts - 12 sts rem at end of row. Turn work.

Next row (RS): Cont with B, p60, Cut B and cont with A, knit to end of row.
Next row (WS): With A, knit all sts.

## BEGIN SHAPING

Next Row (RS): K12, p1, (k2, p2) until 13 sts rem, p1, k12.
Next Row (WS): K13, work in rib as est until 12 sts rem, W&T.
Next Row (RS): Work in rib as est until 12 sts before last W&T (108 sts worked), W&T.
Next Row (WS): Work in rib as est until 12 sts before last W&T (96 sts worked), W&T.
Cont as est until only 12 sts rem to be worked before next W&T.
You should be in the center of the work, on a RS row. Work in rib as est to the last 13 sts, slipping wraps onto needle and working together with wrapped sts, p1, k12.
Next Row (WS): Knit

## EDGE RUFFLE

Next Row (RS): Slip 12 sts onto the RH needle, break A, join B. Purl 120, creating ruffles as per special techniques section. 12 sts rem at end of row. Turn work.
Next row (WS): Knit 120. 12 sts rem unworked at end of row. Turn work.
Next row (RS): Purl 120 sts, k12.

## COLLAR EDGE

You are now at the end of a RS row. Rotate the work 90° so the narrow edge of the piece is ready to be worked. PU 5 sts along this narrow edge by inserting LH needle, traveling from left to right, into each purl bump along edge of work With B, knit these sts.

## EDGE RUFFLE, OPPOSITE SIDE, PART 1

Carefully undo provisional cast on and slip sts onto second circ.

With RS facing, rotate work 90° so that the newly released provisional sts are ready to be worked. With B, k 12, p120, k12.

## OPPOSITE COLLAR EDGE

Rotate work 90°. PU 5 sts as along prev narrow edge. With B, knit these sts.

## BINDING OFF RUFFLE

Rotate work so you have returned to the original set of live sts. K12, p60.

## BO, PART 1

With B, BO as foll: (P2tog, slip resulting st from RH needle to LH needle) rep 72 times until all sts are BO from long edge, 1 st rem on RH needle.

Rotate work so that the 5 edge sts are ready to be worked, slip st from RH needl to LH needle and BO 5 edge sts in the same manner as previous 72 sts.

Rotate work again and BO first 12 sts, purl 120 - 12 sts rem unworked at end of row. Turn work.

Next Row (WS): Knit 120. Turn work.
Next Row (RS): BO all sts as previously worked.

## FINISHING

Weave in ends of A. With a sewing needle and white thread, roll cut ends of B under and hem.

Lay collar Wrong Side up and steam block, paying special attention to sts worked in A. Turn piece over and steam block, fluffing the ruffles.

Sew a 1" button to the non-buttonhole end. Collar may be worn alone, or basted onto the lapel of an existing coat or jacket.

## N-H Ruff Schematic

**Detail of collar ruffles**

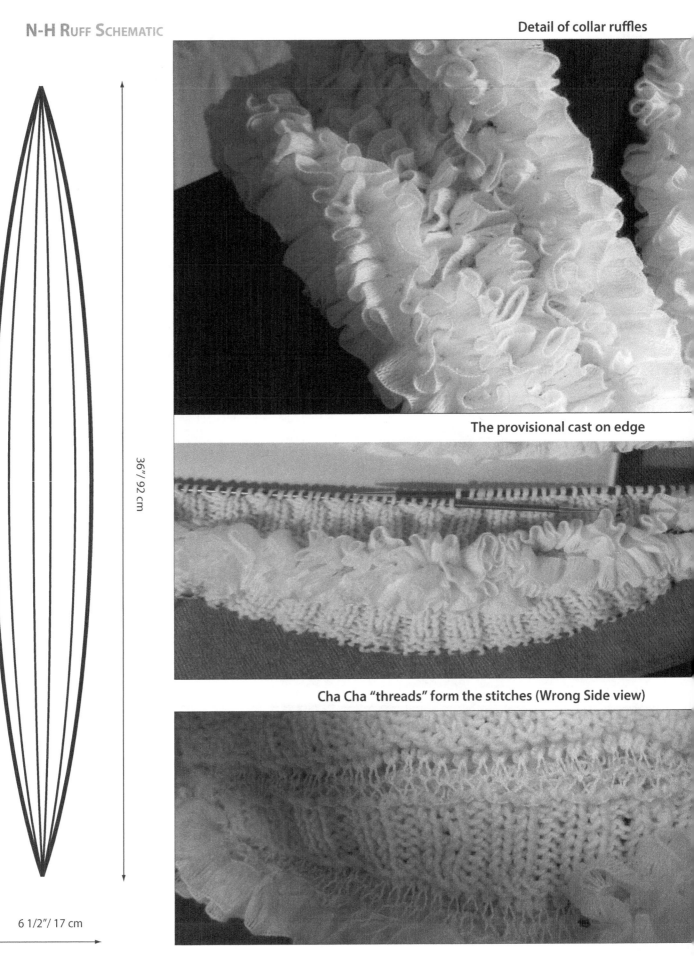

36"/ 92 cm

6 1/2"/ 17 cm

**The provisional cast on edge**

**Cha Cha "threads" form the stitches (Wrong Side view)**

Alexandra Amalie von Bayern
by Joseph Karl Stieler, 1845

Katerina Rosa Botzaris
by Joseph Karl Stieler, 1820

Portrait of Mlle. L.L.
Young Lady in a Red Jacket
by James Tissot, 1864

# Victorian

1820-1905

Maiden Cape

Tissot Bolero

Katarina Jacket

Natalie Fur Collar

Photo Celithemis

Natalie Clifford Barney in Fur Cape
by Alice Pike Barney, c. 1905

The period we know as Victorian, spanning the reign of the British monarch of the same name, lasted roughly from 1837 to the end of the century.

As communication around the world improved, the pace of fashion trends also quickened. Although silhouette details in skirt and shoulder width changed, a firmly corseted figure with a relatively natural (albeit constricted) waistline remained constant throughout the Victorian era and into the first decade of 1900. For the most part, hats and hair styles were worn close to the head (erroneous, anachronistic picture hats from the movie <u>Gone With the Wind</u> notwithstanding) until the explosion of millinery extravaganza in the late nineteenth and early twentieth centuries.

PERNOTTO. COL. SUO. SEGUITO
ALLA. SIBILLA IL. DI 16 MARZO. 1856

**Small and compact like a shrug, the three lace layers of the Maiden Cape hide armholes that keep the garment in place.**
*Background: Sibilla Antico Ristoriante, Tivoli, Italy*
*Maiden Cape modeled by Hannah Landy, knit by Annie Modesitt*

IL · DUCA · REGN
DI · SAXE · GOBUR
FU · ALLA · SIBILLA · LI

FU · AL

MARIA ALEXANDROWNA
D · DI · RUSSIA · ONORO
ALBERGO II 7 GIUGNO

*Garment Photo: Jen Simonson; Background Photo: Annie Modesitt*

# Maiden Cape

Princess Alexandra of Bavaria never married, leading a literate and quiet life as Abbess of the Royal Chapter for Ladies of St. Anne.

Fashions throughout the nineteenth century changed in dramatic ways.

Skirt widths began the century rather narrow, expanded to huge mid-century proportions, drew back to create a soft bustle in the 1870s and a firmer "shelf" bustle in the 1880s, expanding again by 1900.

Waistlines moved up, then down, then *farther* down, then back up to hover at a natural waistline by the end of the century.

But one style remained constant: an evening ball was the one place where a young woman could be – indeed, was *expected* to be – fetchingly naked at the shoulders.

After a day of high necklines, sunset was the perfect time to show off creamy shoulders (and perhaps catch a chill, leading to a romantically disabling bout of consumption). Or, one could wear this three-layered ruffled "shrawl" with shaped armholes, designed to stay firmly in place, during an elegant waltz or a lively polka, and keep the chills at bay.

Photo BOT/Magnus Manske

**Alexandra Amalie von Bayern by Joseph Karl Stieler, 1845 (replica of a 1838 portrait)**

## MAIDEN CAPE INFORMATION

| | |
|---|---|
| Finished Bust | 34 (40) " / 86.5 (102) cm |
| Skill Level | K 3 Intermediate |
| Fiber A | Artyarns, Ultramerino 6 (274yds/250m 3.5oz/100gr) White, 1 ball |
| Fiber B | Artyarns, Beaded Mohair (170yds/155m 1.75oz/50gr) White, 3 balls |
| Fiber C | Mokubu Stitch Warpless Ribbon Ecru & Black, 48"/125cm |
| Gauge | 16 sts x 24 rows in St st in yarn A using needle size: 7 US/4.5mm |
| Needles | Size 7 US/4.5mm |
| Notions | Waste yarn for provisional cast on (smooth & contrasting color), safety pin, size G/4mm crochet hook for button loops & provisional cast on, three ¾"/20mm buttons. |

## MAIDEN CAPE STITCHES

St st – Stockinette Stitch
Rev St st – Reverse St st
YO – Yarn Over
K2tog-R – Knit 2 tog with a right slant
K2tog-L – Knit 2 tog with a left slant
Sl st wyws – Slip st with yarn to the wrong side
Sl st wyrs – Slip st with yarn to the right side

## MAIDEN CAPE TECHNIQUES

Provisional Cast On
K2tog Picot Bind Off

*See Special Techniques, page 116, for full explanations on how to work the stitches and techniques listed above.*

## MAIDEN CAPE LACE RUFFLE

Row 1: P1, YO, k1, YO, p2.
Row 2: K1, p3, k1.
Row 3: P1, YO, k3, YO, p2.
Row 4: K2, p5, k1.
Row 5: P1, YO, k5, YO, p2.
Row 6: K2, p7, k1.
Row 7: P1, YO, k7, YO, p2.
Row 8: K2, p9, k1.
Row 9: P1, YO, k9, YO, p2.
Row 11: YO, k3, k2tog-L, p3, k2tog-R, p3, YO, k1.
Rows 12, 14, 16 & 18: P6, k3, p6.
Row 13: K1, YO, k2, K2tog-L, p3, k2tog-R, k2, YO, k2.
Row 15: K2, YO, k1, k2tog-L, p3, k2tog-R, k1, YO, k3
Row 17: K3, YO, k2tog-L, p3, k2tog-R, YO, k4.

*Note: When above directions are worked in the round for the sleeves, work RS (odd) rounds as written, work even rounds in patt as est, purling the purls and knitting the knit sts and YOs from prev round.*

Next Row (WS): Sl 1 wyws, k1, sl 1 wyws, knit to last 3 sts, sl 1 wyws, k1, sl 1 wyws.
Next row (RS): K1, sl 1 wyrs, k1, k2tog-L, knit to last 3 sts, k1, sl 1 wyrs, k1 — 135 (159) sts

### EST LACE PATTERN

Note: At this point the Right & Wrong sides are reversed, as you work the RS of the lace ruffles, the WS of the body will be facing you. It is helpful to mark the WS with a safety pin so that as you add the lace layers it's obvious at a glance what is the Right and Wrong sides.

### TOP RUFFLE

Row 1 (RS): With B, K1, sl 1 wyrs, k1, p1, work Lace Ruffle Chart row 1 to last 3 sts k1, sl 1 wyrs, k1 — 199 (235) sts
Row 2 (WS): Sl 1 wyws, k1, sl 1 wyws, work Lace Ruffle Chart row 2 to last 4 sts, end k1, sl 1 wyws, k1, sl 1 wyws.
Cont in patts as to Row 18 of chart — 455 (539) sts. Work 2 rows of garter and BO using the K2tog Picot BO (see Special Techniques, page 116)

### MIDDLE RUFFLE

On the Right Side of the work, PU 1 st for each purl bump across the center garter ridge (omit 1 purl bump anywhere in the row), and PU 3 sts each edge — 135 (159) sts.

Arrange work so that the Top Ruffle is hanging to the bottom of the work and the original provisional cast on will be at the top of the work. You are now ready to start a RS row.

With B and starting with Row 5 of the lace chart, est lace patt as foll:

Next Row (RS): K1, sl 1 wyrs, k1, p1, [p1, YO, k5, YO, p2] rep to last 3 sts , end k1, sl 1 wyrs, k1 — 167 (197) sts
Next Row (WS): Sl 1 wyws, k1, sl 1 wyws, [k2, p7, k1] rep to last 4 sts, end k1, sl 1 wyws, k1, sl 1 wyws.
Cont working in lace patt as est, working edge sts as in previous sections to Row 18 of chart — 231 (273) sts. Work 2 rows of garter and K2tog Picot BO as for Top Ruffle

## MAIDEN CAPE

### BODY

With a piece of waste yarn, provisionally cast on 136 (160) sts.

### ARMHOLE PLACEMENT

Next Row: With A, P 23 (27) sts, k 18 (22) sts, p 54 (62) sts, k 18 (22) sts, p 23 (27) sts
Next Row: K 23 (27) sts, p 18 (22) sts, k 54 (62) sts, p 18 (22) sts, k 23 (27) sts

### BODY RIB

Row 1: With A, K1, sl 1 wyrs, k1 (DKSS edge), [p2, k2] rep until 3 sts rem, end p2, k1, sl 1 wyrs, k1 (DKSS edge)
Row 2: Sl 1 wyws, k1, sl 1 wyws, work in rib as est to last 3 sts, sl 1 wyws, k1, sl 1 wyws.
Rep last 2 rows 5 (6) times more — 12 (14) rows of ribbing.

### GARTER BAND

Rows 1 & 3: K1, sl 1 wyrs, k1, knit to last 3 sts, k1, sl 1 wyrs, k1.
Row 2: Sl 1 wyws, k1, sl 1 wyws, knit to last 3 sts, sl 1 wyws, k1, sl 1 wyws.
Row 4: Sl 1 wyws, k1, sl 1 wyws, [k2, p2] rep to last 3 sts, sl 1 wyws, k1, sl 1 wyws.
Return to Body Rib and work 12 (14) more rows of rib once more, end with a RS row.

## Three layers of lace built onto a sleeved, structured garment.

### BOTTOM RUFFLE

Remove waste yarn and slip provisionally cast on sts onto needle so you are ready to work a RS row (same orientation as for Middle Ruffle) — 135 (159) sts (plus a little half stitch, which you can ignore.)

Starting with Row 5 of the lace chart, work bottom ruffle as Middle Ruffle, bind off in the same manner.

## SLEEVES

With wrong side facing (the side opposite the ruffled side), pick up 18 (22) sts from the purl bumps 23 (27) sts in from left edge (bumps will have been isolated in first row of body).

With A, cable cast on 21 (26) sts — 40 (48) sts total. With B knit 1 round, join work, placing marker to note start of round.

Arrange work so the right side (outside) of the sleeve is facing you and work rows 5-18 of the Ruffle Lace Chart. Work K2tog Picot BO as for previous ruffles, repeat for second sleeve.

### TOP EDGE

Row 1 (RS): With B, Pick up & Knit 1 st for each purl bump along top edge of work, above top ruffle. PU 3 sts each edge — 135 (159) sts
Row 2 (WS): Knit all sts.
Row 3 (RS): K2, YO, [k4, YO, k2tog-R] rep 22 (26) times, k1. — 136 (160) sts.
Row 4 (WS): Knit all sts.
Bind off in K2tog Picot Bind Off as for previous ruffles.

## FINISHING

Join a strand of B to the Right Front edge at the top of the bottom ruffle. With crochet hook, chain 12, join back to body and tie off. Repeat at the top of the middle and top ruffles. Sew one ¾"/20mm button to the left front, opposite the formed button loops.

Steam block ruffles and ruffled sleeve using a hand held steamer or the steam setting on an iron.

Lay work flat, Wrong Side Up. Steam from the wrong side, pulling the lace open and allowing each section steamed to dry flat.

Spread sleeve open and flat (see schematic) and with A tack armholes to body at points shown.

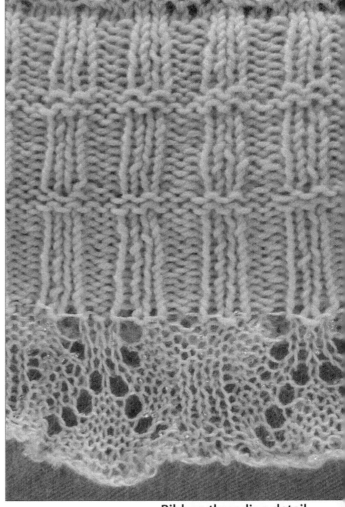

**Ribbon threading detail**

**Button loop detail**

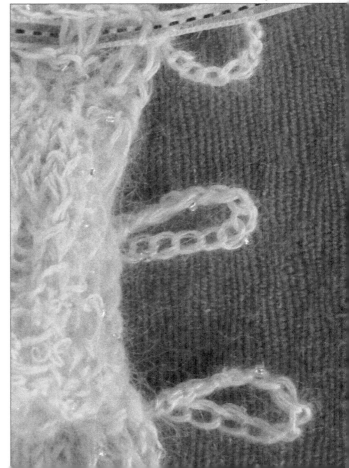

## MAIDEN CAPE SCHEMATIC

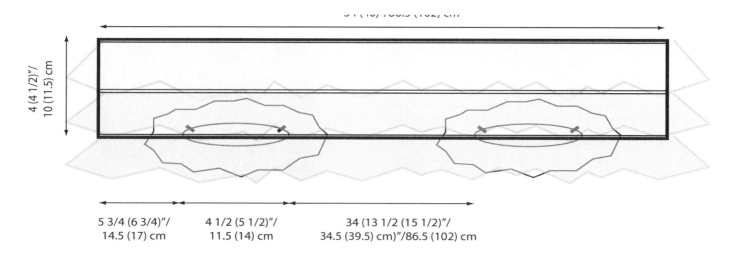

34 (40)/ 86.5 (102) cm

4 (4 1/2)"/
10 (11.5) cm

5 3/4 (6 3/4)"/
14.5 (17) cm

4 1/2 (5 1/2)"/
11.5 (14) cm

34 (13 1/2 (15 1/2)"/
34.5 (39.5) cm)"/86.5 (102) cm

## MAIDEN CAPE LACE RUFFLE CHART

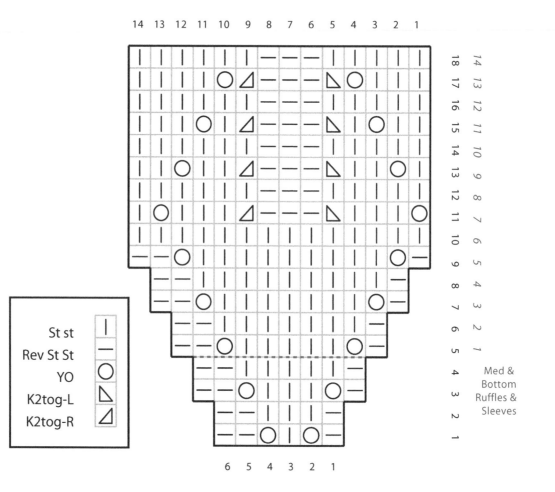

| | |
|---|---|
| St st | │ |
| Rev St St | — |
| YO | ○ |
| K2tog-L | ◁ |
| K2tog-R | ◁ |

Med &
Bottom
Ruffles &
Sleeves

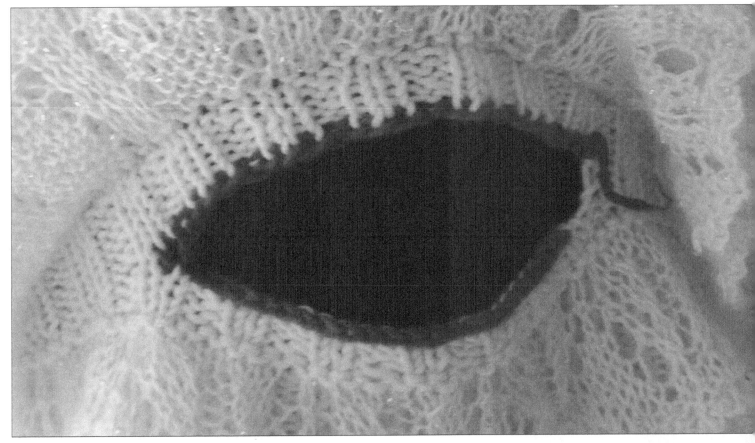

**Armhole opening with waste yarn**

**Armhole opening after lace sleeve has been worked**

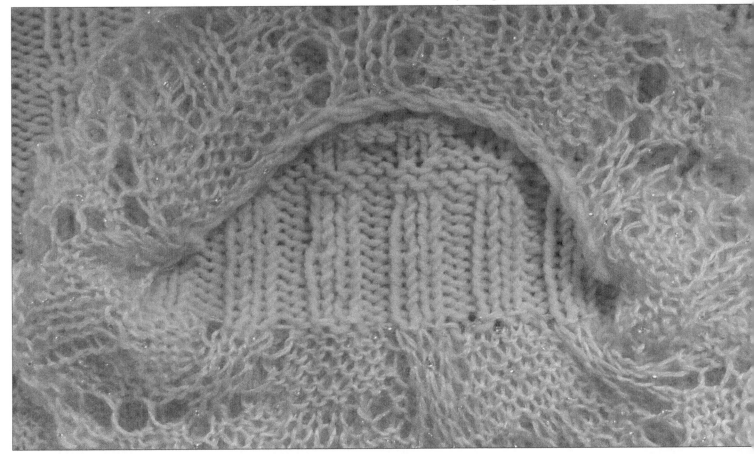

**This twice-felted short jacket is steam blocked and shaped after the final felting for a perfect, "tailor-made" fit.**

*Background: Green Park Allée, London*

*Tissot Bolero modeled by London Nelson, knit by Annie Modesitt*

# Tissot Bolero

Based on a 1864 painting by Tissot, this felted jacket features 3/4 length open sleeves and a cabled / bobbled edge.

There are certain pieces of clothing that just shouldn't work.

They're a little oddball, a little over the top, but somehow the garment has such a sense of *belief* in itself that it makes a cohesive fashion statement.

This felted jacket is one of those.

The pattern shape is an oval, created using short row shaping.

Based on a short *Zouave* jacket – itself inspired by military silhouettes of the period – the unselfconscious use of bobbles is what sets this garment apart from other pieces.

Using a technique I call the I-Bobble (based on the concept of I-Cord) you'll find these bobbles easier to make and better looking than bobbles you may have tried in the past!

Photo-Wikipaintings

**Portrait of Mlle. L.L., Young Lady in a Red Jacket
by James Tissot, 1864**

The trick when felting this garment is to machine wash it twice, then shape it with steam while it is still damp.

Wet wool is malleable; it's possible to mold it, even to the point of wearing it over a T-shirt as it dries so that it fits your figure as perfectly as possible!

## TISSOT BOLERO INFORMATION

| To Fit Bust | 29 (34, 38, 44, 49, 53, 59)"/ 74 (86.5, 97, 112, 125, 135, 150.5) cm |
|---|---|
| Finished Bust | 32 (37, 41, 47, 52, 56, 62)"/81.5 (94.5, 104.5, 120, 132.5, 143, 158) cm |
| Skill Level | K5 Experienced |
| Fiber | Imperial Yarn Pencil Roving (dbl) (200yds/182m 4oz/114gr) Wild Strawberry, 6 (6, 7, 7, 8, 9, 10) sk. |
| Gauge | 12 sts x 20 rows = 4"/10cm UNFELTED in St st using **2 strands of roving** and needle size 10.5US/6.5mm |
| Needle | Size 10.5 US/6.5mm 36" circular needle or two 24" circular needles. |
| Notions | Darning needle, waste yarn, cable needle (optional), washing machine (for felting), steamer or steam iron for blocking. Stitch markers (4 white, 2 blue, 1 red, 1 black) |

## TISSOT BOLERO

### BODY
CO 8 sts.

Row 1: Pfb in each st — 16 sts.
Row 2: Kfb in each st — 32 sts
Row 3: Purl all sts.
Join work and begin working in the round.

*Place markers in the following round in this color order: White, blue, white, red, white, blue, white and a black marker to note start of round (see schematic).*

Round 1: (Grandma Right Inc [GR Inc], k3, pm) 8 times — 40 sts. Place black marker to note start of round.
Round 2 and all even rounds: Knit all sts.
Round 3: (GR Inc into next st, k to the next marker, sm) rep to end of round.
Rep rounds 2 & 3 until there are 24 (28, 32, 36, 40, 44, 48) sts in each section, 192 (224, 256, 288, 320, 352, 384) sts to-

## TISSOT BOLERO STITCHES

St st – Stockinette Stitch
Rev St st — Reverse St st
Sl st wyws – Slip st with yarn to the wrong side
Sl st wyrs – Slip st with yarn to the right side
W&T — Wrap & Turn
K2tog-R – Knit 2 tog with a right slant
K2tog-L – Knit 2 tog with a left slant
K3tog-L – Knit 3 tog with a left slant
P2tog-L – Purl 2 tog with a left slant
Kfb – Knit into the front and back of a stitch
Pfb – Purl into the front and back of a stitch
GR Inc – Grandma Right Increase
GL Inc – Grandma Left Increase
VDD – Vertical Double Decrease
C6R – Cable 6 Right
C6L – Cable 6 Left

*See Special Techniques, page 116, for full explanations on how to work the stitches and techniques listed above.*

tal. End with an odd (increase) round.

### ARMHOLE PLACEMENT
*Armholes will be placed in sections 3 and 6 (see schematic)*

Next Round: Knit all stitches in the first 2 sections, stop at blue marker. With a piece of waste yarn knit all stitches in third section. Slip these waste yarn sts back onto LH needle.
With main yarn knit these waste yarn stitches. Continue on across next 2 sections, stop at the white marker (you are at section 6).

With a second piece of waste yarn work all the stitches in section 6 as for section 3, slipping them back and re knitting the waste yarn stitches.

Knit to end of round.

### FIRST SHORT ROW SECTION
Take a moment and look at your circular piece of knitting with 8 markers; the black marker notes the bottom of the piece, the red marker the top.

Begin working First Short Row Section at the black marker as foll:

Short Row 1 (RS): [GR Inc, k to the next marker, sm] 4 times, to red marker. Short Row 2 (WS): W&T, purl 2 stitches before start of round.
Short Row 3: (Knit to next marker, GR Inc, k to next marker, slip marker) 3 times, work to 2 sts before W&T from prev RS row.
Short Row 4: W&T, purl back to 2 sts before W&T from prev WS row.
Rep short rows 3 & 4 for a total of 12 (14, 16, 18, 20, 22, 24) rows, increasing in the first stitch after each marker on RS rows (see note below) and working a W&T 2 sts before each prev W&T as est until there are 2 (3, 2, 2, 3, 2, 2) sts on either side of the blue marker. End with a WS row.
Next Row: Knit to red marker, increasing in the first stitch after each marker as est and slipping wraps onto needle and working tog with wrapped sts. You are now at the red marker.
*Note There will be an inconsistent number of stitches in each section with 32 (37, 42,*

## CABLE BOBBLE EDGE

Row 1 (RS): K1, sl 1 wyrs, k1 (DKSS edge), k1, p1, k1, W&T.
Row 2: Sl wrapped st, k1, p1, k1, sl 1 wyws, k1, sl 1 wyws (DKSSe).
Row 3: DKSS edge, k1, p1, k1, k6, W&T.
Row 4: Sl wrapped st, p6, k1, p1, k1, DKSS edge.
Row 5: DKSS edge, k1, p1, k1, k6, p3, k3tog-L.
Row 6: Sl dec st, k3, p6, k1, p1, k1, DKSS edge.
Row 7: Make Bobble in first st, sl 1 wyrs, k2, p1, k1, C6L, p3, k2tog-L.
Row 8: Rep row 6.

48, 53, 58, 64) sts in sections 2-4, 26 (30, 34, 39, 43, 47, 52) sts in section 1

### CONTINUE FIRST SHORT ROW SECTION
Continuing around work, repeat First Short Row Section, this time working from the red marker to the black marker — 32 (37, 42, 48, 53, 58, 64) sts in sections 2-4 & 6-8, 26 (30, 34, 39, 43, 47, 52) sts in sections 1 & 5, 244 (282, 320, 366, 404, 442, 488) sts total.

Knit 1 row, slipping wraps onto needle and working along with each wrapped stitch.

### PLAIN SECTION
Work 4 (4, 4, 6, 6, 6, 8) rounds, increasing at each marker as est in every other round — 36 (41, 46, 54, 59, 64, 72) sts in Sections 2-4, 6-8, 30 (34, 38, 45, 49, 53, 60) sts in Sections 1 & 5 – 276 (314, 352, 414, 452, 490, 552) sts.

There will be no further increasing from this point.

### SECOND SHORT ROW SECTION
Knit 1 round even, slipping wraps onto needle and working tog with wrapped sts..

Short Row 1: Knit to second white marker (after blue marker)
Short Row 2: W&T, purl back past blue marker to 2 sts before white marker.
Short Row 3: W&T, knit past blue marker to 2 sts before W&T from prev RS row.
Short Row 4: W&T, purl back to 2 sts before W&T from prev WS row.
Rep short rows 3 & 4 for a total of 6 (8, 8, 10, 10, 12, 14) rows. End with a WS row. Knit to red marker.

### CONTINUE SECOND SHORT ROW SECTION
Continuing around work, repeat Short Rows 1-4 to match opposite side.

Knit to black marker (end of round).

### CABLED BORDER
Turn work so that WS is facing. Using a piece of waste yarn and any provisional cast on method you choose, cast 15 sts onto the LH needle.

With main yarn est the first WS row of the cabled border across the prov CO sts as foll:

Next Row (WS): K3, p6, k1, p1, k1, Sl 1 wyws, k1, Sl 1 wyws. Turn work.
You are now at the outer (DKSS) edge of the cabled border, ready to work a RS row. You will be working toward the last round worked.

Working from written or charted instructions as you prefer, work cabled edging, joining border to circumference by decreasing first sts of garment in rows 5 & 7.

## TISSOT BOLERO TECHNIQUES

DKSS Edge – Double Knit Slip Stitch Edge
Provisional Cast On
MB – Make Bobble
Kitchener Stitch

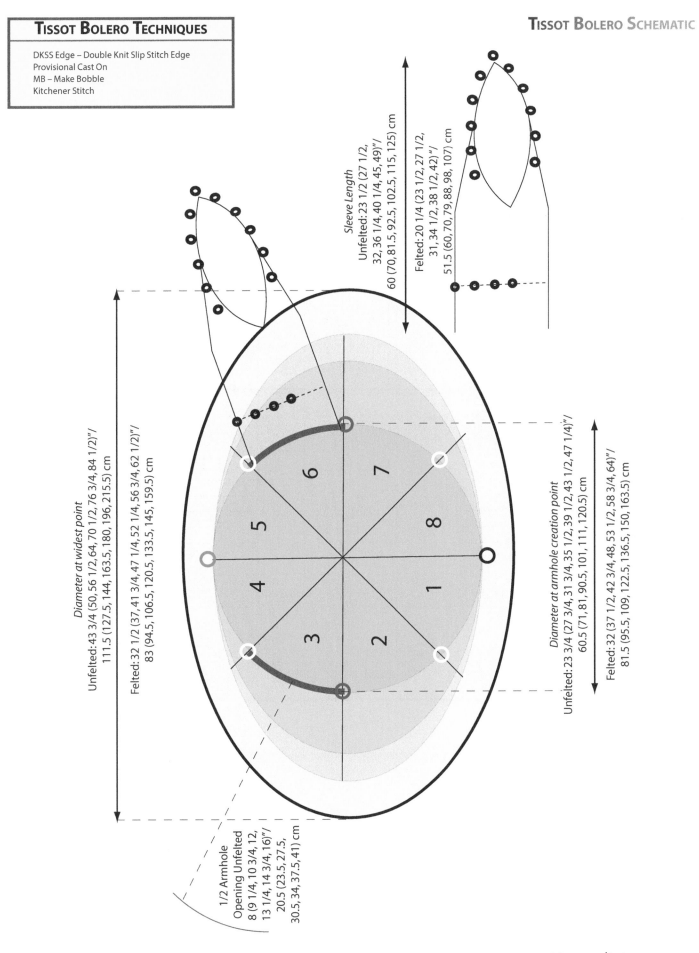

*Sleeve Length*
Unfelted: 23 1/2 (27 1/2,
32, 36 1/4, 40 1/4, 45, 49)"/
60 (70, 81.5, 92.5, 102.5, 115, 125) cm
Felted: 20 1/4 (23 1/2, 27 1/2,
31, 34 1/2, 38 1/2, 42)"/
51.5 (60, 70, 79, 88, 98, 107) cm

*Diameter at widest point*
Unfelted: 43 3/4 (50, 56 1/2, 64, 70 1/2, 76 3/4, 84 1/2)"/
111.5 (127.5, 144, 163.5, 180, 196, 215.5) cm
Felted: 32 1/2 (37, 41 3/4, 47 1/4, 52 1/4, 56 3/4, 62 1/2)"/
83 (94.5, 106.5, 120.5, 133.5, 145, 159.5) cm

*Diameter at armhole creation point*
Unfelted: 23 3/4 (27 3/4, 31 3/4, 35 1/2, 39 1/2, 43 1/2, 47 1/4)"/
60.5 (71, 81, 90.5, 101, 111, 120.5) cm
Felted: 32 (37 1/2, 42 3/4, 48, 53 1/2, 58 3/4, 64)"/
81.5 (95.5, 109, 122.5, 136.5, 150, 163.5) cm

1/2 Armhole
Opening Unfelted
8 (9 1/4, 10 3/4, 12,
13 1/4, 14 3/4, 16)"/
20.5 (23.5, 27.5,
30.5, 34, 37.5, 41) cm

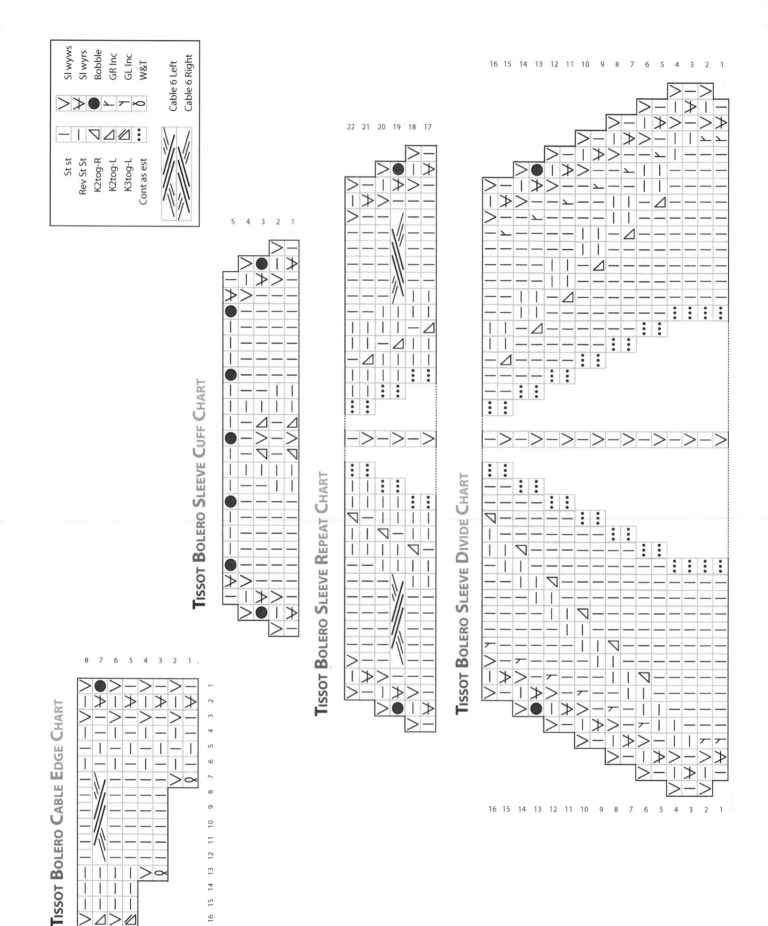

**TISSOT BOLERO CABLE EDGE CHART**

**TISSOT BOLERO SLEEVE CUFF CHART**

**TISSOT BOLERO SLEEVE REPEAT CHART**

**TISSOT BOLERO SLEEVE DIVIDE CHART**

Sl wyws
Sl wyrs
Bobble
GR Inc
GL Inc
W&T

Cable 6 Left
Cable 6 Right

St st
Rev St St
K2tog-R
K2tog-L
K3tog-L
Cont as est

Repeat the 8 rows of the chart, decreasing 3 sts of garment body circumference for every 8 rows of edging worked.

Work around entire circumference until no stitches remain to be decreased and you have returned to the start of the cabled edge.

Using the Kitchener stitch, 3 needle BO or any joining method you prefer, carefully remove waste yarn and join the CO row to the last row worked.

## RIGHT SLEEVE

Carefully undo the waste yarn at the Right armhole and slip exposed stitches onto circ needle. Use 2 circular needles or several dpns if desired to make the sleeve easier to work.

Arrange the work so that you are at the top of the armhole opening (between sections 5 & 6), place black marker to note start of round — 47 (55, 63, 71, 79, 87, 95) sts total on needle. Join yarn and join

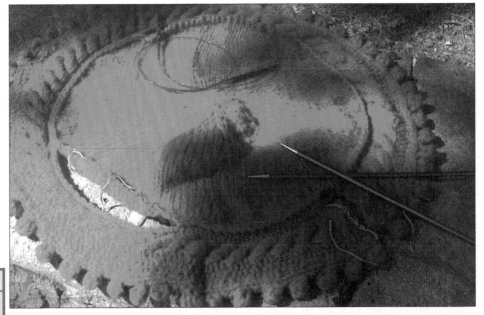

**Shrug body in process, armholes divided onto waste yarn & circulars**

### SLEEVE DIVIDE CHART

Row 1 (RS): K1, sl 1 wyrs, GL Inc, knit to 1 st before white marker, sl 1 (center back st), knit past black marker (remove marker), knit to last 3 sts, GR Inc, sl 1 wyrs, k1.
Row 2 (WS): [Sl 1 wyws, k1, Sl 1 wyws] (DKSS edge),GL Inc, purl to last 4 sts, GR Inc, DKSS edge.
Row 3: [K1, sl 1 wyrs, k1] (DKSS edge), p1, work to last 4 sts, slipping center st (white marker) as est, end p1, DKSS edge.
Row 4: DKSS edge, k2, p to last 5 sts, k2, DKSS edge.
Note: from this point shaping will take place at the start of EVERY row, there will be no shaping at the end of the rows.
Row 5: DKSS edge, GL Inc, p2, k2tog-L, work in patt as est to last 5 sts, p2, DKSS edge.
Row 6: DKSS edge, GL Inc, k2, p2tog, work to last 6 sts, k2, p1, DKSS edge.
Row 7: DKSS edge, GL Inc, k1, p2, k2tog-L, work in patt as est to last 6 sts, p2, k1, DKSS edge.
Row 8: DKSS edge, GL Inc, p1, k2, p2tog, work in patt as est to last 7 sts, k2, p2, DKSS edge.
Row 9: DKSS edge, GL Inc, k2, p2, k2tog-L, work in patt as est to last 7 sts, p2, k2, DKSS edge.
Row 10: DKSS edge, GL Inc, k2, p2, p2tog, work in patt as est to last 8 sts, k2, p3, DKSS edge.
Row 11: DKSS edge, GL Inc, k3, p2, k2tog-L, work in patt as est to last 7 sts, p2, k4, DKSS edge.
Row 12: DKSS edge, GL Inc, p3, k2, p2tog, work in patt as est to last 8 sts, k2, p4, DKSS edge.
Row 13: MB, sl 1 wyrs, k1, GL Inc, k4, p2, k2tog-L, work in patt as est to last 7 sts, p2, k5, sl 1 wyrs, MB.
Row 14: DKSS edge, GL Inc, p4, k2, p2tog, work in patt as est to last 8 sts, k2, p5, DKSS edge.
Row 15: DKSS edge, GL Inc, k5, p2, k2tog-L, work in patt as est to last 7 sts, p2, k6, DKSS edge.
Row 16: DKSS edge, GL Inc, p5, k2, p2tog, work in patt as est to last 8 sts, k2, p6, DKSS edge.

### SLEEVE DECREASE CHART

Rows 17 & 21: DKSS edge, k6, p2, k2tog-L, work in patt as est to last 11 sts, p2, k6, DKSS edge.
Rows 18, 20 & 22: DKSS edge, p6, k2, p2tog, work in patt as est to last 11 sts, k2, p6, DKSS edge.
Row 19: MB in first st, sl 1 wyrs, k1, C6R, p2, k2tog-L, work in patt as est to last 11 sts, p2, C6L, k1, sl 1 wyrs, MB

for working in the round.

Round 1: Knit 12 (14, 16, 18, 20, 22, 24) sts, place white marker (sleeve back), knit until 12 (14, 16, 18, 20, 22, 24) sts rem before start of round, place red marker (sleeve front), knit to end of round.
Round 2: Knit all sts
Round 3: Knit to white marker, sm, slip next st, knit to red marker, sm, slip next st, knit to end of round.
Rep last 2 rounds until piece meas 7 (8¼, 9¾, 11, 12¼, 13¾, 15)"/18 (21, 25, 28, 31.5, 35, 38.5) cm, ending with Round 3.

### BOBBLE ROUND
Work to 1 st before red marker. [MB, k4 (5, 5, 6, 7, 7, 8) sts] six times (working past black marker), then knit around to start of round.

Resume rounds 2 & 3, starting with round 3, repeating these rounds until sleeve meas 7 (8¼, 9¾, 11, 12 ¼, 13¾, 15)"/18 (21, 25, 28, 31.5, 35, 38.5) cm from bobble row (or desired length — lengthen or shorten here. Work to red marker.

### SLEEVE DIVIDE
From this point you will be working back and forth in rows, increasing at the beg and end of rows 1 & 2, and at the beg only from row 5 to the last row.

Work 16 rows of the Sleeve Divide Chart, working from or written instructions or chart as you prefer.

### SLEEVE DECREASE REPEAT
Working from Sleeve Repeat Chart or written instructions as you prefer, rep rows 17-22 until 27 sts rem.

### SLEEVE CUFF
Work 5 rows of the Sleeve Cuff Chart, working from or written instructions or chart as you prefer. After finishing Row 5, work 3 rows in St st, then bind off all sts loosely. Sew bound off edge to WS of work, folding cuff hem at bobble row (turning ridge).

### FINISHING & FELTING

Weave in ends. This garment will need a good amount of felting, I found that two cycles in a front loading washing machine was sufficient. After running the garment through one hot/warm wash cycle remove from washer and assess the size/shape. If you feel it needs to be smaller, more compact, return to washer for another cycle. **DO NOT MACHINE DRY!**

After the final wash cycle, remove the garment and asses the measurements. This is the point when you will SCULPT the jacket. Using a hand held steamer or an iron with a steam setting, inundate the area of the garment you need to reshape.

For example, the sleeve may be slightly too short and too narrow at the upper arm area. Steam one sleeve liberally at the upper arm, and while the garment is very warm and damp, use your hands to pull and mold the sleeve to the desired shape.

When wool is wet and warm, you can stretch and mold it pretty easily. Take full advantage of these malleable properties to work your garment to the shape and size you desire.

You may find you spend more time steaming the garment than you did felting it, but remember that the shape the garment cools and dries in is the shape it retains. When the garment is just about the shape/size you want, put it on and wear it while it dries for a 'tailor-made' fit.

### CUFF CHART

Row 1 (RS): DKSS edge, k6, p2, k2tog-L, sl 1, k2tog-R, p2, k6, DKSS edge.
Row 2 (WS): DKSS edge, p6, k2, p3, k2, p6, DKSS edge.
Row 3: MB, sl 1 wyrs, k7, p1, k2tog-L, sl 1, k2tog-R, p1, k7, sl 1 wyrs, MB.
Row 4: DKSS edge, p6, k1, p3, k1, p6, DKSS edge.
Row 5: K1, sl 1 wyrs, [MB, p3] 4 times, MB, sl 1 wyrs, k1.

**Mixing two yarns with different weights in this garment creates a fabric with matching stitch and row gauges. This allows for beautifully matching colorwork seams.**

*Background: Canterbury Cathedral Exterior*

*Katarina Jacket modeled by Lisa Pannell, knit by Annie Modesitt*

*Garment & Background Photo: Annie Modesitt*

# Katarina Jacket

Katarina Rosa Botsari, a great beauty of her time, married Prince George Karatzas four years after this portrait was painted.

There are some painters who capture clothing so beautifully that they become favorites of costume historians. Joseph Karl Stieler is, for me, one of these most *sartorially* helpful artists.

His painting here of Katarina (daughter of Greek Independence war hero Markos Botsari) shows her in a romanticized interpretation of a national Greek costume, popularized by Queen Amalia.

The heavily embroidered velvet jacket is fur-trimmed and is worn over a loosely pleated dress.

I've moved the pleats to the jacket cuffs and left them at a 3/4 length *(which can be easily modified to full length if you wish)* and I have interpreted the embroidery as all-over colorwork.

**Katerina Rosa Botzaris**
**by Joseph Karl Stieler, 1820**

I've used two vastly different Trendsetter yarns (a worsted thickness, lightweight *ribbon* and a sport thickness, densely cabled rayon/polyester yarn.)

Serendipitously, this mixing of two yarn weights works, in this case, to create a fabric with similar stitch and row gauges. This allows for wonderful pattern matching at row/stitch seams.

## KATARINA JACKET INFORMATION

| To Fit Bust | 32 (36, 41, 47, 53, 59)"/81.5 (92, 104.5, 120, 135, 150.5) cm |
|---|---|
| Finished Bust | 36 (40, 45, 51, 57, 63)"/92 (102, 115, 130, 145.5, 160.5) cm |
| Skill Level | K 4 Advanced |
| Fiber A | Trendsetter Valentina Ribbon (126yds/115m 1.75oz/50gr) 78% Poliammide, 22% Cotone Mako Honeycomb, 7 (8, 11, 14, 18, 21) balls |
| Fiber B | Trendsetter Sunshine 75% Rayon, 25% Polyester (95yds/87m 1.75oz/50gr) Chocolate , 6 (8, 10, 13, 16, 19) balls |
| Gauge | 24 sts x 26 rows = 4"/10cm when worked in charted pattern using both yarns, 20 sts = 4"/10cm when worked in ribbing using only Sunshine on size 8US/5mm needle. |
| Needle | 8US/5mm 36" Circular (add'l size: 7US/4.5mm ) |
| Notions | Stitch holders, darning needle, sewing needle, thread, hook & eye, 18 (18, 23, 23, 28, 27")/45.5 (46, 58.5, 58, 70, 69.5) cm separating zipper (or length to match finished piece, it's wisest to purchase this after garment is complete)optional size 5US/3.75mm needles for collar. |

## KATARINA JACKET STITCHES

St st – Stockinette Stitch
Rev St st – Reverse St st
VDD – Vertical Double Decrease
K2tog-R – Knit 2 tog with a right slant
K2tog-L – Knit 2 tog with a left slant
Kfb – Knit into front & back of stitch
Pfb – Purl into front & back of stitch

## KATARINA JACKET TECHNIQUES

PU & K – Pick up and knit

*See Special Techniques, page 116, for full explanations on how to work the stitches and techniques listed above.*

# KATARINA JACKET

## BODY

### GARTER/RIB WAISTBAND
With largest needle and A, CO 110 (122, 138, 158, 174, 194) sts

Row 1 (RS): [K2, p2] rep to last 2 sts, , k2.
Row 2: [P2, k2] rep to last 2 sts, , p2.
Work 7 more rows of ribbing as est, end with a RS row.
Row 10 (WS): Knit all sts.
Row 11: Repeat Row 1.
Rows 12-13: Work in rib as est
Row 14: Knit all sts
Rep Rows 11-14 twice more
Row 23: Repeat Row 1
Rows 24-33: Work in rib as est
Row 34: Knit all sts.

### BODY INCREASE
Change to smallest needle and Yarn B

Next Row: K2 (2, 2, 4, 2, 4) sts, kfb into each stitch across row to last 2 (2, 2, 4, 2, 4) sts, k2 (2, 2, 4, 2, 4) sts — 216 (240, 272, 308, 344, 380) sts
Next Row (WS): Knit all sts.
Next Row (RS): Purl all sts
Rep last 2 rows once more, then work 1 more WS row — 6 rows of Rev St st total.

### EST CHARTED COLOR WORK PATTERN
With Medium needle and Yarn A, and beg with row 15 (7, 31, 23, 11, 7) and st 5 (25, 25, 7, 5, 19) of colorwork chart, rep sts 1-32 of chart 6 (7, 8, 9, 10, 11) times, then work chart once more, ending with st 28 (8, 8, 26, 28, 14) .

Work in patt as est to row 32, then rep 32 rows of chart 1 (1, 2, 2, 2, 2) times more. Piece should meas approx 7 (8, 9¾, 10¾, 12¼, 13¼)"/18 (20.5, 25, 27.5, 31.5, 34) cm from start of colorwork. Cut yarn.

### DIVIDE FRONTS & BACK
Slip 60 (72, 72, 90, 92, 110) sts from either end onto stitch holder to work later. The rem 96 (96, 128, 128, 160, 160) sts will form the back.

### BACK
Rejoin yarn to start of 96 (96, 128, 128, 160, 160) Back sts, cont in patt as est, work until Back length meas 8 (8, 10¾, 10¾, 13¼, 13¼)"/20.5 (20.5, 27.5, 27.5, 34, 34) cm from armhole divide, or desired body length.

### SHOULDER SHAPING
Next 2 Rows: BO 10 (10, 13, 13, 16, 16) sts at start of row (armhole edge), work in patt as est to end of row.
Next 2 Rows: BO 10 (10, 13, 13, 17, 17) sts at start of row, work in patt as est to end of row.
Next 2 Rows: BO 10 (10, 14, 14, 17, 17) sts at start of row, work in patt as est to end of row.
Slip rem 36 (36, 48, 48, 60, 60) sts for the Back Neck to a stitch holder to work later.

**A zipper closure makes this a very versatile and slightly edgy jacket.**

**Colorwork Chart**

## FRONTS
Slip Front sts onto needle and establish separate sources of yarn for each Front. Work both Fronts at the same time in patt as est until Fronts meas 5¾ (5, 8¼, 7, 10¼, 9)"/14.5 (13, 21, 18, 26, 23) cm from armhole divide.

## NECK SHAPING & SHOULDER JOIN
Bind off 10 (14, 10, 16, 14, 20) sts from each neck edge once, then BO 4 from each neck edge every other row 3 (4, 3, 5, 4, 6) times, then BO 2 st at each neck edge every other row 4 (6, 5, 7, 6, 8) times, AND AT THE SAME TIME when Front armhole depth matches Back, shape shoulders as directed for Back. Join shoulders using any method you prefer.

## SLEEVES
With the smallest needle and yarn A, and starting at the center bottom of underarm, PU&K 96 (96, 128, 128, 160, 160) sts around Left Armhole. Join, place marker to note start of round.

Change to larger needle. Beg with St 1, Row 15 of chart, work around all sleeve sts, matching colorwork patt to body sts as est. Note: Because of the unusual gauge properties of using these two dramatically different weight yarns together, the rows and stitches should match up one to one.

## SLEEVE DECREASE
Work to Row 32 of chart, then beg dec at underarm as foll:

Round 1: Slip 1st st, work in patt as est to 2 st before marker, VDD (remove marker) – 94 (94, 126, 126, 158, 158) sts
Round 2 and All Even Rounds: Work in patt as est.
Round 3: Slip 1st st, work in patt as est to1 st before prev dec, VDD – 92 (92, 124, 124, 156, 156) sts
Rep last 2 rounds, decreasing 2 sts every other

round until a total of 16 decrease rounds have been worked — 32 sts have been decreased and the colorwork pattern is continuous around sleeve – 64 (64, 96, 96, 128, 128) sts

## UPPER ARM
Cont working as est in patt with no further dec until sleeve meas 8 (8½, 8½, 9, 9½, 9½)"/20.5 (21.5, 21.5, 23, 24, 24) cm from shoulder.

## ELBOW
Change to smallest needle and Yarn B.

Round 1: Knit all sts
Rounds 2-5: Purl all sts
Change to Yarn A.
Round 1: Knit all sts
Round 2: [K2, p2] 16 (16, 24, 24, 32, 32) around
Rep last round 15 times more, 16 rounds total.
Change to Yarn B.

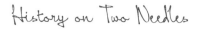

Round 1: Knit all sts.
Rounds 2-5: Purl all sts.
Change to largest needle and return to Yarn A.
Round 1: Knit all sts.
Round 2: [K2, p2] 16 (16, 24, 24, 32, 32) times
Rep last round until entire sleeve meas 16 (17, 17, 18, 19, 19)"/41 (43.5, 43.5, 46, 48.5, 48.5) cm from shoulder seam for a three-quarter sleeve lengh, or to desired length.
Bind off all sts loosely.

### PLACKETS & COLLAR BAND

With RS facing and a single strand of B and smaller needles, PU&K 106 (108, 138, 136, 165, 163) sts along Left Front edge, pm, PU&K 94 (104, 122, 134, 152, 164) sts around the neck, pm, PU&K 106 (108, 138, 136, 165, 163) sts down the Right front edge – 306 (320, 398, 406, 482, 490) total.

Row 1(WS): Purl to marker, sm, pfb, p to 1 st before next marker, pfb next st, sm, purl to end of row – 308 (322, 400, 408, 484, 492) sts.
Row 2 (RS): Knit to first marker, sm, kfb next st, k to 1 st before next marker, kfb next st, sm, k to end of row –310 (324, 402, 410, 486, 494) sts.
Repeat last 2 rows once – 314 (328, 406, 414, 490, 498) sts.
Next Row (WS): Knit all sts.
Next Row (RS): Knit to marker, sm, VDD, knit to 3 sts before next marker, VDD, sm, knit to end of row – 310 (324, 402, 410, 486, 494) sts.
Next Row (WS): Purl all sts.
Rep last 2 rows twice more – 302 (316, 394, 402, 478, 486) sts.

Bind off all sts.

### FINISHING

Weave in ends. Steam block piece, fold placket and collar band at rev st st row and stitch bound off edge to WS. Steam block hemmed collar and placket again.

Baste zipper into place on WS of placket fronts, hand or machine sew zipper to placket. Sew hook & eye at top placket edge to close jacket collar.

### OPTIONAL ROLLED COLLAR

Return to the rev st st ridge on the neckline. With RS facing and a single strand of B and size 5US/3.75mm needles, PU 94 (104, 122, 134, 152, 164) sts along top of neckband.

Next Row (WS): Purl.
Next Row (RS): Knit.
Rep last 2 rows until a total of 6-10 rows have been worked. BO all sts and allow collar to roll.

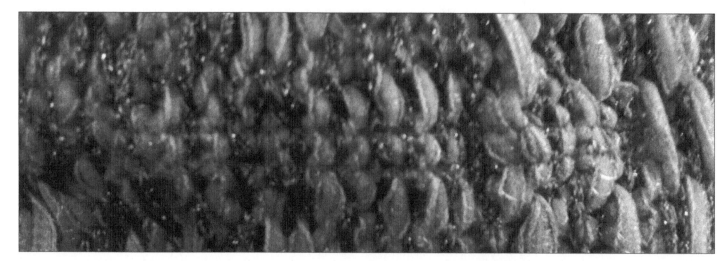

**I knit the body of my garment in the round, then steeked the center front. You can do this, or choose to knit it flat.**

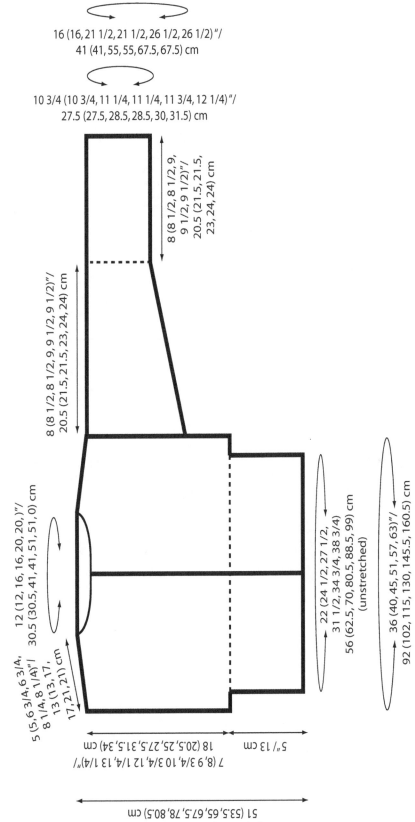

16 (16, 21 1/2, 21 1/2, 26 1/2, 26 1/2)"/
41 (41, 55, 55, 67.5, 67.5) cm

10 3/4 (10 3/4, 11 1/4, 11 1/4, 11 3/4, 12 1/4)"/
27.5 (27.5, 28.5, 28.5, 30, 31.5) cm

8 (8 1/2, 8 1/2, 9, 9 1/2, 9 1/2)"/
20.5 (21.5, 21.5, 23, 24, 24) cm

8 (8 1/2, 8 1/2, 9, 9 1/2, 9 1/2)"/
20.5 (21.5, 21.5, 23, 24, 24) cm

12 (12, 16, 16, 20, 20,)"/
30.5 (30.5, 41, 41, 51, 51, 0) cm

5 (5, 6 3/4, 6 3/4,
8 1/4, 8 1/4)"/
13 (13, 17,
17, 21, 21) cm

22 (24 1/2, 27 1/2,
31 1/2, 34 3/4, 38 3/4
56 (62.5, 70, 80.5, 88.5, 99) cm
(unstretched)

36 (40, 45, 51, 57, 63)"/
92 (102, 115, 130, 145.5, 160.5) cm

7 (8, 9 3/4, 10 3/4, 12 1/4, 13 1/4"/
18 (20.5, 25, 27.5, 31.5, 34) cm

5"/ 13 cm

20 (21, 25 1/2, 26 1/2, 30 1/2, 31 1/2"/
51 (53.5, 65, 67.5, 78, 80.5) cm

Used to mimic the drape and fall of a fur cape, *Splash* novelty eyelash yarn is given a new sophistication in this graceful wrap.

*Background: Canterbury Cathedral Interior*

*Natalie Fur Cape modeled by Hannah Landy, knit by Annie Modesitt*

*Garment Photo: Jen Simonson, Background Photo: Annie Modesitt*

# Natalie Fur Cape

*There are no bad yarns, just bad uses for misunderstood yarns. Eyelash yarn falls into the "most misused" category.*

Throughout history, fur has traveled from being a fabric of necessity, to a wearable show of strength, to a fashion statement of conspicuous consumption.

Ultimately, fur is a luxurious and sensual experience. But for a variety of reasons, many women will never own a fur cape.

No one would mistake Natalie Barney for anyone but a woman of style and power.

And no one will mistake the Natalie Fur Cape as anything but a sensational piece of faux fur. And that's a great deal of its charm!

The pattern involves short row shaping to create the "pelts" and the use of two colors for contrasting purposes.

But there's no reason to restrict yourself to naturalistic coloring in your garment!

This is meant to be a fun garment, a lark, a warm cloak that makes you and those around you smile a bit when you don it.

Make it your own, choose your colors and have a GREAT time knitting it up!

*Photo by Chris 73*

**Natalie Clifford Barney in fur cape
by Alice Pike Barney
c. 1905**

## NATALIE FUR CAPE INFORMATION

| | |
|---|---|
| Size | One Size |
| Total length | 21"/ 54cm |
| Skill Level | K 2 Easy |
| Fiber | Crystal Palace, Splash |
| | (85yds/78m 3.5oz/100gr) |
| | Color A - Jaguar 7181, 3 balls |
| | Color B - Black 202, 1ball |
| | Color C - Sable 7185, 2 balls |
| Gauge | 8 sts x 10 rows = 4"/10cm in St st |
| | using needle size: 10US/6mm |
| Notions | Darning needle |

## NATALIE FUR CAPE STITCHES

St st – Stockinette Stitch
Rev St st – Reverse St st
W&T – Wrap and Turn
K2tog-L – Knit 2 tog with a left slant

*See Special Techniques, page 116, for full explanations on how to work the stitches and techniques listed above.*

## NATALIE FUR CAPE SCHEMATIC

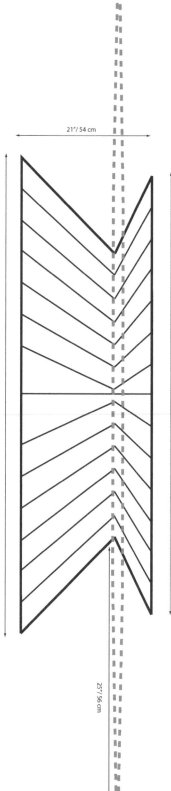

21"/ 54 cm

68"/172 cm

38"/98 cm

25"/ 56 cm

## FUR CAPE

### BODY

With A, cast on 42 sts. Knit 4 rows (garter st)

Next Row (RS): With B, k24, place yarn marker with long tail, knit to end of row
Next Row (WS): Knit, slipping marker.

### BEGIN SHORT ROW PELTS

Slip marker when necessary, allowing long tail to mark the neckline of the stole as you work the 18 pelts that make up the body.

Rows 1, 3 & 5: With A, Knit to the end of the row.
Row 2: K3, p14, W&T.
Row 4: K3, p28, W&T.
Row 6: K3, p to the end of the row.
Rows 7 & 9: K9, W&T.
Rows 8 & 10: Purl to the end of the row.
Rows 11, 13 & 15: Knit to the end of the row.
Row 12: K3, p28, W&T.
Row 14: K3, p14, W&T.
Row 16: K3, p to the end of the row.
Rows 17 & 18: Change to B and Knit all sts.

Rep Rows 1-18 12 times more, then with A work 4 rows in Garter. Bind off all sts loosely.

### "TAIL" TIES

Cast on 50 sts. With sts on working needle, PU 75 along yarn marker line of body (red dotted line on schematic), picking up 4 sts for every 5 rows, then cast on 50 more sts — 175 sts total.

Next row: K50, [k2tog, k1] 50 times, k50.
Next row: K2tog, knit to 2 sts before end of row, k2tog.
Rep last row 8 times – 132 sts.
Next row K2tog, purl to 2 sts before end of row, k2tog.
Next row: K2tog, k to 2 sts before end of row, k2tog.
Rep last row 8 times – 112 sts.
Next Row: Knit all sts. Cont in garter for a total of 12 rows or until "tails" are desired width. BO all sts very loosely.

### FINISHING

With a darning needle weave in ends. Lightly steam block piece if necessary.

**The Natalie Fur Cape in process next to a beaver pelt at the Minnesota Historical Society.**

# Specials

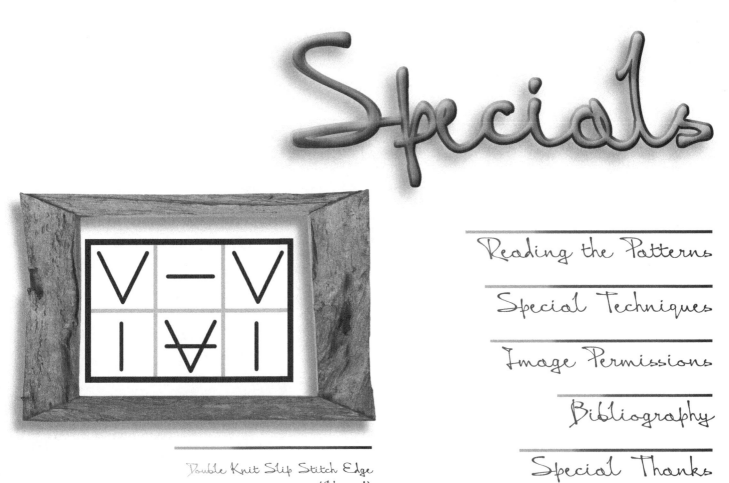

Double Knit Slip Stitch Edge
(Charted)

Here is the necessary, back-of-book information that makes every knitting book complete.

I've included an extra chapter here: Reading The Patterns. Please take a moment to look over this chapter; I think it will help all knitters, whatever their level of experience, to enjoy this book to the fullest!

Dog in a Basket on a Bike
by the Metro in Paris

Settling in for an afternoon of knit design and tea
at Di Gilpin's Bothy, Fife, Scotland

# Reading the Patterns

*I've tried to make the patterns and charts as clear and easy to use as possible. Here are some tips to help it all make sense.*

I tend to knit differently than many folks, and I've discovered that I think about patterns differently than some other designers, too. In order to make the experience of using this book as pleasant and rewarding as possible, I thought I'd highlight some of the different charting and pattern shortcuts that I like to use.

## CHARTS

### WRITTEN TEXT

I adore charts, but I understand that not everyone thinks in a visual manner. To that end, I've written out the text for most of the charts in the book. The charts that haven't been translated into text are either very straightforward (and therefore simple to read) or are portions of charts which have been explained in previous rows or within the pattern so that subsequent chart rows should be clear.

Even if you're someone who feels you don't *like* charts, I urge you to open yourself up to the possibility that charts can be a source of comfort, allowing you to visualize motifs in ways that text will not allow.

Use the chart text, while stopping every few rows to compare your work to the charts. Slowly, there will begin to be a connection. Remember, a chart is a *symbolic* representation of the <u>right side</u> of the knitted work.

### REPEATING MOTIFS

When a motif repeats within a chart I've outlined it with a strong blue line. In many cases I've broken it out from the non-repeating stitches by giving it a much lighter background. Generally I've numbered *only repeating sections*.

### NON-REPEATING STITCHES

If there are stitches in a motif that are <u>only worked once</u> and not repeated across the row, these are shown in a light or medium grey.

### CONT AS ESTABLISHED

I'll use the symbol … in some patterns when I want you to continue working the row (or series of rows) as established.

### STITCH MARKERS

When I feel it's helpful, I'll use a colored line to note stitch marker placement.

### SHADING

Often in complex charts I'll shade certain areas to help isolate them from each other. I do this for clarity. I hope you find it helpful.

## TERMINOLOGY

### SLIPPING STITCHES

For clarity, I choose to use the phrase, "Slip 1 Stitch with Yarn to Wrong Side" (wyws) or "Slip 1 with Yarn to Right Side" (wyrs). This means that as you're slipping a stitch, you will hold the yarn to the side of the work (RS or WS), which is designated by the instructions.

I prefer this to the phrase, "Slip 1 with Yarn to Front" because, depending on whether the RS or WS is facing you, the "front" may change.

### DKSS EDGE

This Double Knit Slipped Stitch (DKSS) edge is much easier than it seems. It's one of the most useful edges I know, and I use it quite a bit.

The main thing to remember when working the DKSS Edge is that every time you slip a stitch within the edge the yarn is held TOWARD you, regardless of whether the WS (wrong side) or RS (right side) is facing you.

Whenever the DKSS edge is shown in a chart, it will be a medium grey color.

### INCREASING

Like decreases, increases have a left and right slant. I like to use this directional movement in my patterns. One increase I enjoy quite a bit is something I call a *"Grandma"* increase. Basically this simply means knitting or purling into the stitch <u>below</u> the next stitch on the needle (the grandma stitch) and <u>also</u> knitting the stitch above the grandma stitch. Whether one knits the grandma first (GR Inc – Grandma Right Inc) or knits the stitch above grandma first (GL Inc – Grandma Left Inc) determines which way the increase will slant.

Please see Special Techniques, page 116, for step by step instructions on how to work any of the techniques.

### DECREASING

When you work 2 stitches together as a decrease, they will slant to the left or to the right. The traditional K2tog slants to the right, the techniques known as SSK (slip, slip knit), SKP (slip 1, knit 1, pass slipped st over) and K2tog-tbl (knit 2 together through the back loop) are all variations on K2tog-L, knitting 2 stitches together so they slant to the left. For this reason I prefer to use the phrases, *K2tog-L* and *K2tog-R* instead of SSK and K2tog.

To think of this a different way, when you insert your working (right) needle into 2 stitches to create a standard k2tog, note that the tip of the working needle is pointing to the RIGHT as it enters the stitches. This tells you that these stitches will slant to the **right** when they are worked together.

Alternatively, when working an SSK or a K2tog-tbl, note that the tip of the working needle enters the stitches pointing to the LEFT, noting a **left**-slanting decrease.

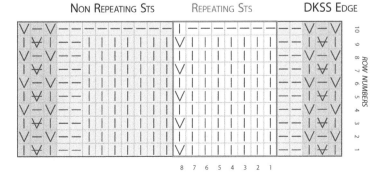

# Special Techniques

| Chart Symbol | Stitch or Technique Name | Description |
|---|---|---|
| | | **Terms & Abbreviations (Knit & Crochet)** |
| | **Blo** <br> **Back loop only** | Work into the back loop only of the stitch as it sits, regardless of whether the right or wrong side of work is facing you. |
| | **Flo** <br> **Front loop only** | Work into the front loop only of the stitch as it faces you, regardless of whether the right or wrong side of work is facing |
| | **PM** | Place Marker |
| | **PU** <br> **Pick Up** | Insert needle into stitch, creating a new loop on the needle out of the existing fabric. No new source of yarn is used for a simple PU. |
| | **PU&K** <br> **Pick up & Knit** | Insert needle into next stitch, stabbing all the way from the right side to the wrong side of the work. Wrap a loop around the needle, pull the loop through, creating a knit stitch. |
| | **SM** | Slip Marker |
| | **Wyrs** <br> **With yarn right side** | With yarn to right side (public side) of work |
| | **Wyws** <br> **With yarn wrong side** | With yarn to wrong side (private side) of work |
| | | **Special Stitches (Crochet)** |
| | **B-Hdc** <br> **Bead half double crochet** | YO hook, insert hook in st, push bead up the thread as close to RS of work as possible, YO, draw yarn through stitch, YO, draw yarn through the three loops on hook. |
| | **B-Sc** <br> **Bead single crochet** | Insert hook in st, push bead up the thread as close to RS of work as possible, YO, draw yarn through stitch, YO, draw yarn through the two loops on hook. |
| | **Ch** <br> **Chain** | YO, draw yarn through loop on hook. |
| ⊤ (boxed) | **Dc** <br> **Double Crochet** | YO hook, insert hook in st, YO hook, draw yarn through stitch, YO hook, draw yarn through first 2 loops on hook, YO hook, draw yarn through rem 2 loops on hook. |
| ⊤ (boxed) | **Hdc** <br> **Half Double Crochet** | YO hook. Insert hook in the next stitch to be worked. YO hook. Pull yarn through stitch. YO hook. Pull yarn through all 3 loops on hook (one half double crochet made). |
| ✕ (boxed) | **Sc** <br> **Single Crochet** | Insert hook in stitch. YO hook. Pull yarn through stitch. Yarn over. Pull yarn through 2 loops on hook (one single crochet made). |
| | **SC2 Tog** | [Insert hook into next st, YO] twice (three loops on hook), YO, draw loop through all loops on hook. |
| | **DC2 Tog** | [YO hook, insert hook in st, YO hook, draw yarn through stitch] twice (five loops on hook), YO hook, draw yarn through first 3 loops on hook, YO hook, draw yarn through rem 3 loops on hook. |

| Chart Symbol | Stitch or Technique Name | Description |
|---|---|---|
| | | Special Stitches (Knit) |
| | **B6L** Braid 6 Left | K2, sl 2 sts and hold to front, k2, k slipped sts. |
| | **B6R** Braid 6 Right | Move yarn to RS, sl 2 sts & hold to backk2, k slipped sts, k2. |
| | **C3L** Cable 3 sts with a Left twist | Sl 2 sts & hold t.o front, k2, k slipped sts |
| | **C3R** Cable 3 sts with a Right twist | Move yarn to RS, sl 2 sts & hold to back k2, k slipped sts. |
| | **C4L** Cable 4 sts with a Left twist | Sl 2 sts & hold to front, k2, k slipped sts. |
| | **C4R** Cable 4 sts with a Right twist | Move yarn to RS, sl 2 sts & hold to back k2, k slipped sts. |
| | **C6L** Cable 6 sts with a Left twist | Sl 3 sts & hold to front, k3, k slipped sts. |
| | **C6R** Cable 6 sts with a Right twist | Move yarn to RS, sl 3 sts & hold to back k3, k slipped sts. |
| | **DS** Dipstitch | Draw loop through stitch several rows (as directed) below next st and work tog with next st on needle.<br><br>If pulled tight this can create a puckered effect; if left relaxed it forms an effect like a crocheted 'spike stitch' |
| | **DKSS** Double Knit Slipped St Edge 5 St DKSS 6 St DKSS | RS Row: K1, wyrs sl1, k1, work to last 3 sts, k1, wyrs sl1, k1<br>WS Row: wyws sl1, k1, wyws sl1, work to last 3 sts, wyws sl1, k1, wyws sl1<br><br>*Note: When working this edge you will ALWAYS hold the yarn toward YOU when slipping sts. In some patterns an additional 'gutter' of Reverse St sts is inserted between the DKSS edge and the main fabric. These are described as 5 St DKSS or 6 St DKSS Edge and included in the charts for these patterns.* |
| | **GL inc** Grandma Left Increase | Knit next st, do not slip off needle. Insert needle into st immediately below st just knit and knit that st, slip both sts off left needle, creating a left-slanting inc. |
| | **GPL inc** Grandma Purl Left Increase | Purl next st, do not slip off needle. Insert needle purlwise into st immediately below st just purled and purl that st, slip both sts off LH needle, creating a left-slanting inc. |

| CHART SYMBOL | STITCH OR TECHNIQUE NAME | DESCRIPTION |
|---|---|---|
| (symbol: K with dot) | **GPR INC** GRANDMA PURL RIGHT INCREASE | Insert needle purlwise into st immediately below next st and purl that st, purl next st on needle, slip both sts off needle, creating a right-slanting inc. |
| (symbol: Y shape) | **GR INC** GRANDMA RIGHT INCREASE | Knit into st immediately below next st on needle, then knit next st on needle, creating a right-slanting inc. |
| (symbol: left triangle) | **K2TOG-L** KNIT 2 TOGETHER WITH A LEFT SLANT | Knit 2 sts together so the working needle is pointing to the left as it enters the stitch (dec will slant to the left) aka SSK, k2togTBL or skp. |
| (symbol: right triangle) | **K2TOG-R** KNIT 2 TOGETHER WITH A RIGHT SLANT | Knit 2 sts together so the working needle is pointing to the right as it enters the stitch (dec will slant to the right) aka k2tog |
|  | **KFB** K INTO FRONT & BACK | Knit into the front and back of one stitch, then slip that stitch off the needle. (Increase of 1 st.) |
|  | **KFBF** KNIT IN FRONT, BACK & FRONT AGAIN | Knit into the front and back of one stitch, then knit into the front again slipping stitch off the needle. (Increase of 2 sts.) |
| (symbol: filled circle) | **MB** MAKE BOBBLE | 1. K3 sts into next st by kKfbf,[Slip these 3 sts back to LH needle]. 2. Kfb into first st, k1, Kfb into last st, [Slip these 5 sts back to LH needle]. 3. Kfb into first st, k1, Kfb into last st, [Slip these 7 sts back to LH needle]. 4. Knit 1 row (optional), k2, VDD, k2, [Slip these 5 sts back to LH needle]. 5. K1, VDD, k1, [Slip these 3 sts back to LH needle], VDD. |
| (symbol: left triangle with °) | **P2TOG-L** PURL 2 TOGETHER WITH A LEFT SLANT. | Purl 2 sts together so they slant to the left <u>when viewed from the right side of the work.</u> |
| (symbol: right triangle with °) | **P2TOG-R** PURL 2 TOGETHER WITH A RIGHT SLANT | Purl 2 sts together so they slant to the right <u>when viewed from the right side of the work.</u><br><br>The working needle is pointing to the right as it enters the sts (needle enters the 2nd st on LH needle, then 1st st on LH needle) aka P2tog TBL (through the back loop) |
|  | **PFB** P INTO FRONT & BACK | Purl into the front and back of one stitch, then slip that stitch off the needle (Increase of 1 st.) |
| (symbol: horizontal dash) | **REV ST ST** REVERSE ST ST | Purl on the right side of the work, knit on the wrong side of the work. |
| (symbol: V) | **SL 1 WYWS** SLIP STITCH | With yarn to wrong side of work, insert RH needle purlwise (unless otherwise directed) into st and slip off of LH needle. *This is the default for slipping stitches; slip this way unless otherwise directed.* |
| (symbol: inverted V / A) | **SL 1 WYRS** SLIP STITCH | With yarn to right side of work, insert RH needle purlwise (unless otherwise directed) into st and slip off of LH needle. |
| (symbol: vertical line) | **ST ST** STOCKINETTE STITCH | Knit on the right side of work, Purl on the wrong side of work. |
| (symbol: inverted V) | **VDD** VERTICAL DOUBLE DECREASE | Sl 2 sts as if to work k2 tog-R, k1, pass slipped sts over (decrease of 2 sts) |

| Chart Symbol | Stitch or Technique Name | Description |
|---|---|---|
| Y (symbol) | **VDI** **Vertical Double Increase** | K into front of st, YO, k into back of st |
| (W&T symbol) | **W&T** **Wrap & Turn** | Slip next st to RH needle, wrap yarn around base of stitch and return to LH needle. Turn work and begin working back in the opposite direction from the previous row. |
| O | **YO** **Yarn Over** | Wrap yarn around hook or needle |

### Special Techniques (Knit & Crochet)

**3-Needle Bind Off (aka 'binding off together')**
1. Place the two pieces on knitting needles so the right sides of each piece are facing each other with the needles parallel.
2. Insert a third needle one size larger through the leading edge of the first stitch on each needle (knitwise)
3. Knit these stitches together as one, leaving 1 st on RH needle.
4. Repeat steps 2 & 3 and slip older stitch on LH needle over newer stitch.
Repeat step 4 until all sts are bound off. Cut yarn, pull through last stitch.

**Cable Cast On**
Slip needle between 1st & 2nd sts on LH needle and pull loop through to front. Slip this loop onto the LH needle twisting it clockwise (in other words, 'back' the stitch onto the left needle.)

Repeat, each time using the newly created stitch as first stitch on LH needle.

**Cha Cha Ruffle**
To create a ruffle with Cha Cha yarn, use the 'thread edge' of the ribbon yarn as the working yarn, using one square, or cell, for each stitch. Insert needle into next stitch on needle, grab the thread from the next 'cell' and pull this through the existing stitch on needle. Note: When working in St st, the ruffles will show on the PURL SIDE of the fabric.

**DCE Decorative chain embroidery**
Setup: Holding the yarn at the back of the work, insert the crochet hook from the front to the back.
1. YO, draw loop through to the front of the fabric.
2. (Move hook to point where next chain should start and insert from the front to the back. YO, draw loop through fabric and through loop on hook.)
3. Repeat, moving the hook at the start of each new stitch to create a decorative pattern on the front of the fabric.
4. End by drawing the last loop through to the WS of the work, pull the tail through the loop, tie off.

**I-Cord Bind Off**
Setup: Cast on 2 sts at start of row using Cable Cast On.
1. K2, K2tog-L.
2. Slip 3 sts from RH needle back onto LH needle.
3. Pull yarn taut across back of work.
Repeat steps 1-3 across work until 3 sts rem, K3tog-L.

**K2tog Picot BO**
[(K1, sl st back onto LH needle) once, k2tog-L, sl st back onto LH needle], rep across all sts until only 1 st rem, pull tail through loop. For a larger picot loop, increase the number of times the original stitch is knit and returned to the LH needle.

**Kitchener Stitch**
To prepare, break yarn leaving a tail 3 times the length of the seam, thread tail through a darning needle.

Place pieces to be joined with WS together and hold both needles in the left hand. Move the stitches toward the points of the needles to make manipulation easier.
1. FRONT NEEDLE: Draw the tail through the 1st stitch on the front needle as if to purl, but do not slip stitch off needle.
2. BACK NEEDLE: Draw yarn through the 1st stitch on the back needle as if to knit, but do not slip stitch off needle.
3. FRONT NEEDLE: Draw tail through the 1st stitch on the front needle as if to knit, slip stitch off needle.
4. FRONT NEEDLE: Draw tail through the 2nd stitch on the front needle as if to purl, do not slip stitch off of needle.
5. BACK NEEDLE: Draw tail through the 1st stitch on the back needle as if to purl, slip stitch off needle.
6. BACK NEEDLE: Draw tail through the 2nd stitch on the back needle as if to knit, do not slip stitch off of needle.
7. Repeat steps 3-6 until all stitches are joined. It is important to maintain an even tension in each stitch as you work as this method can be difficult to undo.

| CHART SYMBOL | STITCH OR TECHNIQUE NAME | DESCRIPTION |
|---|---|---|
| PROVISIONAL CAST ON | | This is a term used to describe a Cast On which can be easily removed later, leaving a row of live stitches to be slipped onto a needle and worked.<br><br>One favorite method is to crochet a chain in waste yarn with at least as many sts as you would like to cast on. Tie off the end of the chain, placing a knot in the tail. Slip your knitting needle into the bump at the back of each chain, creating a "stitch" on the needle.<br><br>When desired, the chain can be loosened and pulled off at the knotted end. |
| PL<br>PICOT LOOP 7 ST | | Ch 7, [sc into fourth chain from hook, ch 7], end ch 3. |
| TC<br>TWISTED CORD | | 1. Measure a length of yarn 4 times longer than desired length of final twisted cord.<br>2. Fold the strand in half and make a slipknot at the cut ends.<br>3. Pass the slipknot over a doorknob and stand far enough away so that the yarn hangs in midair and does not touch the ground.<br>4. Slip a pencil into the slipknot you are holding in your hand and pull the cord taut so that the pencil rests perpendicular to your fingers, allowing the to slip between your middle and pointer finger.<br>5. Begin turning the pencil—similar to the way that the propeller on a toy plane twists a rubber band—to twist the strands of yarn.<br>6. Continue twisting until the yarn is quite taut and evenly twisted. When relaxed slightly the twisted yarn should want to kink up.<br>7. Still holding one end of the yarn in your left hand, with your right hand pinch the twisted strand midway between yourself and the doorknob.<br>8. Bring the ends of the yarn together by moving toward the doorknob, but DO NOT LET GO OF THE MIDDLE OF THE TWISTED YARN. When the 2 slipknots are together you can release the middle of the cord, you will notice the yarn will twist around itself forming a plied cord.<br>9. Still holding tight to the slipknot ends, loose the yarn end from the doorknob and tie both ends together.<br>10. Run an index finger between the cords to even out the twists if necessary. |

## YARNS USED IN THIS BOOK

**MEKETRE SKIRT & TOP**
Elsebeth Lavold Yarns
Knitting Fever International
www.knittingfever.com
PO Box 336
315 Bayview Avenue
Amityville, NY 11701
516-546-3600

**KNOSSOS SHRUG &**
**MINOAN SURPLICE**
Mango Moon Yarns
www.mangomoonyarns.com
Mango Moon Yarns
308 West Main Street, Suite 303
Owosso, Michigan 48867
989-723-5259

**CHITON**
The Buffalo Wool Company
thebuffalowoolco.com
802-379-WOOL (9665)
sales@thebuffalowoolco.com

**SUTTON HOO HELM**
Hazel Knits
www.hazelknits.com

**LADY MARGARET SCARF (I)**
Henry's Attic
www.henrysattic.com
845-783-3930

**LADY MARGARET SCARF (II)**
Muench Yarns, Inc.
www.muenchyarns.com
1323 Scott Street
Petaluma, CA 94954-1135
800-733-9276
info@muenchyarns.com

**WOODSTOCK TUNIC &**
**BLACK PRINCE HOOD**
Berroco, Inc.
www.berroco.com
1 Tupperware Dr. Suite 4,
N. Smithfield, RI 02896-6815
401-769-1212
info@berroco.com

**PEMBROKE JACKET**
Tilli Tomas
www.tillitomas.com
617-524-3330

**GLORIANA JACKET &**
**MAIDEN CAPE**
Artyarns
www.artyarns.com
70 Westmoreland Ave
White Plains, NY 10606
914-428-0333

**FALKLAND SKIRT, ADMIRAL ANJA HAT,**
**NOTTINGHAM HOYLE RUFF & KATARINA JACKET**
Trendsetter Yarns
www.trendsetteryarns.com
16745 Saticoy Street #101
Van Nuys, CA 91406
818-780-5497
information@trendsetteryarns.com

**TISSOT BOLERO**
Imperial Stock Ranch Yarn
www.imperialyarn.com
92462 Hinton Road
Maupin, OR 97037
541-395-2507
contact@imperialyarn.com

**NATALIE FUR CAPE**
Crystal Palace Yarns
www.straw.com
160 23rd Street
Richmond, CA 94804
cpyinfo@straw.com

Sacred

the memory of

MACNAMARA Esq

et in this City who departed

year 1800. Aged 54 years

# Image Permissions

The images in this book are used with permission as described below.

| Page | Image Permission |
|------|------------------|
| **Ancient** | |
| 8 | Snake goddess from the Palace of Knossos, Crete. by an unknown artist, is a Wikipedia and Wikimedia Commons image from the user Chris 73, and is freely available at http://commons.wikimedia.org/wiki/File:Snake_Goddess_Crete_1600BC.jpg under the CC BY-SA 3.0 license. |
| 8 | Caryatid from the Erechtheion, Greece displayed at the British Museum) by an unknown artist, is a Wikipedia and Wikimedia Commons image from the user Marie-Lan Nguyen, and is freely available at http://en.wikipedia.org/wiki/File:Caryatid_Erechtheion_BM_Sc407.jpg under the CC BY-SA 2.5 license. |
| 9 | Offering Bearer Statue by an unknown artist, is a Statue from Egypt, Upper Egypt; Thebes, Southern Asasif, Tomb of Meketre, and is used with permission ©The Metropolitan Museum of Art. Image source: Art Resource, NY . |
| 10 | Background: Egyptian carving on column in Philae temple by Boonsom, is a stock image from Dreamstime, ©Boonsom \| Dreamstime.com. |
| 29 | The Charioteer of Delphi, 470s B.C. Bronze, 5ft.11in. high. Delphi Museum, Greece. by an unknown artist, is a Wikipedia and Wikimedia Commons image from the user RaminusFalcon, and is used with permission http://upload.wikimedia.org/wikipedia/commons/9/9a/AurigaDelfi.jpg under the terms of the GNU Free Documentation License, Version 1.2 or any later version published by the Free Software Foundation. |
| **Medieval** | |
| 34 | Edward of Woodstock, The Black Prince, Funeral Effigy at Canterbury Cathedral by an unknown artist,©Annie Modesitt |
| 34 | Sutton Hoo Helmet (displayed at the British Museum) by an unknown artist, is a Wikipedia and Wikimedia Commons image from the user geni, and is freely available at http://en.wikipedia.org/wiki/File:Sutton_hoo_helmet_room_1_no_flashbrightness_ajusted.JPG under the CC BY-SA 2.0 license. |
| 35 | Possibly Lady Margaret Beaufort, mother of Henry VII, grandmother of Henry VIII, Margaret, and Mary Tudor by an unknown artist, is a Flickr image from lisby1, and is freely available at http://www.flickr.com/photos/60861613@N00/3798032021/ under the CC BY-SA 3.0 license. |
| 37 | Sutton Hoo Helmet (displayed at the British Museum) by an unknown artist, is a Wikipedia and Wikimedia Commons image from the user geni, and is freely available at: http://en.wikipedia.org/wiki/File:Sutton_hoo_helmet_room_1_no_flashbrightness_ajusted.JPG under the CC BY-SA 2.0 license. |
| **Renaissance** | |
| 60 | Unknown man, formerly thought to be Charles Howard, 1st Earl of Nottingham by an unknown artist, is a painting from The National Portrait Gallery, London, and is used with permission ©National Portrait Gallery, London. |
| 60 | The Gripsholm Portrait, though to be Elizabeth I of England by an unknown artist, is a Wikipedia and Wikimedia Commons image from the user PKM, and is freely available at: http://en.wikipedia.org/wiki/File:Gripsholm_Elizabeth.jpg within the Public Domain. |
| 60 | James I of England and VI of Scotland as an 8-year old child, holding a falcon. by Rowland Lockey (attributed) after Arnold Bronckorst, is a painting from The National Portrait Gallery, London, and is used with permission ©National Portrait Gallery, London. |
| 61 | Portrait thought to be of Anne Boleyn, probably a later copy of an image of about 1534 by an unknown artist, is a Wikipedia and Wikimedia Commons image from the user Egore, and is freely available at: http://en.wikipedia.org/wiki/File:Anneboleyn2.jpg within the Public Domain. |
| 74 | Embroidered bookbinding, The Miroir or Glasse of the Synneful Soul by Elizabeth Tudor, is a Wikipedia and Wikimedia Commons image from the user PKM, and is freely available at: http://en.wikipedia.org/wiki/File:Embroidered_bookbinding_Elizabeth_I.jpg published in the US before 1923 and public domain in the US.. |

| Page | Image Permission |
|------|------------------|

# Bibliography

| Publication | Author | Publisher | Date |
|---|---|---|---|
| **Clothing Specific** | | | |
| The Tudor Tailor: Reconstructing Sixteenth-Century Dress | Ninya Mikhaila & Jane Malcolm-Davies | Costume and Fashion Press | ©2006 |
| Patterns of Fashion 4: The Cut and Construction of Linen Shirts, Smocks, Neckwear, Headwear and Accessories for Men and Women C. 1540-1660 | Janet Arnold | Costume and Fashion Press | ©2008 |
| Patterns of Fashion 3: The Cut and Construction of Clothes for Men and Women C1560-1620 | Janet Arnoldw | Costume and Fashion Press | ©1985 |
| Patterns of Fashion 2: Englishwomen's Dresses and Their Construction C.1860-1940 | Janet Arnold | Costume and Fashion Press | ©1977 |
| Patterns of Fashion 1: Women's Clothing 1660-1860 | Janet Arnold | Costume and Fashion Press | ©1977 |
| Nineteenth Century Fashion in Detail | Lucy Johnson | V&A Publishing | ©2009 |
| Fashion (Taschen 25th Anniversary) | Akiko Fukai, Tamami Suoh, Miki Iwagami, Reiko Koga, and Rie Nii | Taschen | ©2007 |
| Pattern Magic 2 | Tomoko Nakamichi | Laurence King Publishers | ©2011 |
| Women's Work: The First 20,000 Years: Women, Cloth, and Society in Early Times | Elizabeth Wayland Barber | W. W. Norton & Company | ©2005 |
| Prehistoric Textiles: The Development of Cloth in the Neolithic and Bronze Ages with Special Reference to the Aegean | Elizabeth Wayland Barber | Princeton University Press | ©1992 |
| 20000 Years of Fashion | Francoise Boucher | Harry N. Abrams | ©1987 |
| The Cut of Women's Clothes: 1600-1930 | Norah Waugh | Routledge | ©1968 |
| Corsets and Crinolines | Norah Waugh | Routledge | ©1990 |
| **Historical Reference** | | | |
| The Ancient Egyptians | Jill Kamil | The American University in Cairo Press | ©1997 |
| The History of England from the Accession of Edward VI. to the Death of Elizabeth (1547-1603) | A. F. Pollard | Longmans Green | ©1911 |
| Spectacle, Pageantry, and Early Tudor Policy | Sydney Anglo | Clarendon Press | ©1997 |
| Bible and Sword: England and Palestine from the Bronze Age to Balfour | Barbara Tuchman | Ballantine Books | ©1956 |
| Britain's Royal Families: the Complete Genealogy | Alison Weir | Pimlico | ©1996 |
| The Stripping of the Altars: Traditional Religion in England, | Eamon Duffy | Yale University Press | ©2005 |
| A Day in the Life of Ancient Rome | Alberto Angela | Europa Editions | ©2007 |
| Women in Ancient Greece | Sue Blundell | Harvard University Press | ©1995 |
| The Lives of the Kings and Queens of England | Antonia Fraser | University of California Press | ©2000 |
| A Needle In The Right Hand of God | R. Howard Bloch | Random House | ©2006 |
| 1066 | Andrew Bridgeford | Walker & Company | ©2006 |
| A World Lit Only By Fire | William Manchester | Little, Brown and Company | ©1993 |

# Special Thanks

A book is never a solo endeavor, special thanks are due to so many folks. This book took several years to complete, and in that time my tally of kind friends grew and grew. And so, In no specific order, here are my thanks:

Many thanks are due to the brilliant writers of social and fashion history and the underrepresented fields of "women's work."

Thank you to my knitting group here in Minnesota who encouraged me as I worked through the completion of my project. Thank you to all of my students who have ooh'd, ahh'd and offered helpful suggestions on the projects in the book when I dragged each one out of my suitcase during classes.

Thank you to Brenda Barnes who helped me wade through the ins and outs of legal image use, and thank you to Nancy Gould for introducing us.

Thank you to Jen Simonson for her lovely model photography, Di Gilpin for her brilliant Scottish tour and Miriam Tegels for her speedy and expert knitting!

Thank you to the museums and suppliers of art, and to Wikimedia and all of the wonderful users there who make the creative commons work for small publishers and designers!

Thank you to Shannon Okey & Cooperative Press for taking care of the bits I hate. Thank you to Kate Atherley, Donna Druchunas, and Elizabeth Green Musselman for their kind and thorough editing.

Thank you to the Yarn Pirates in NJ, who encouraged me when I came up with this crazy idea!

Thank you to every yarn company that supported me in realizing my vision. Without yarn support, designers cannot do great work; a model of symbiosis!

Finally, very great thanks are due to my family for their patience as I left for weeks at a time teaching and taking pictures in far flung locations, only to return home and sit for hours hunched over knitting needles or a computer keyboard, fending off their offers of food with a growled, *"I'm in math HELL!"* I love you, Gerry, Hannah & Max!

Thank you to everyone who supported this project through Kickstarter, giving me the financial boost I needed.

Myrna Stahman, Patti Skinner, Sarah Eyre, Kathy Berkel, Rosi Faiola Reeder, A. McDonald, Laura Col, Nancy McCarthy, Tom Treat, B.M. Hamersma, Harriet Shafran, Ruby Cruse, Patricia Walters, Ellen Silva, Robin Mayfield, Shelly Duniphin, Lisa Pannell, Marie-France Hough, Jean Babbage, Shel Kennon, Sarah Jane Humke, Sasha, Jess Faber, kemoser, London Nelson, Michelle Toich Anderson, hep1013, Amy O'Neill Houck, Jenn Ridley, Paula Durrant, Jennifer Dumas, Brenda Fry, Cathy Cooper, Margaret Shyne Bensen, monder, Samantha Gillett, Veronica Van, Becka Rahn, Sue Krekorian, Victoria Blum Mothes, Kelly Eells, Denise Bell, Stacey Trock, Sara Delano Moore, Debra G. Fox, Eliza Marie Sheppard, William Blanchard, Deborah Robson, Mary McMahon, Jill Wright, Beth Raymond, Mary Ann Nester, Jody Herriott, K.J. Rasmussen, Carol Gould, Tracey Villani, Audrey Lavine, J. Patience, Todd Showalter, Minnie, Stella Gimmestad, Elizabeth Boily, Karl Okerholm, Diane Ellis, Melanie, Linda Rockwell, Susan, Susan Druding, Cindy Moore, Suzanne Wells, Lea Bennett, Regina Imhoff, Debby Accuardi, Joycelyn Poon, Elizabeth Risch, Barbara Eady Colvin, Rose White, Janet McNeil, Ricki Seidman, M.D. Smith, Jerre, Astor Tsang, Melissa Gaul, Ruth Velasco-Schmitz, Colleen LaMotte, Silver Hart, Deirdre Kennedy, Nicole Bishop, Deborah Weiland, Christine Stevenson, Gretchen Greene, Susan Crawford, Lori Sievert, Larisa Harris, Elizabeth Callahan, Jan Ollila, Kathy Igo, Eve Mudrinich, Amy C. Rutter, Meg Dotseth, Allison Miller Henle, Elizabeth W. Detmold, Merrie Davidson, lyndau, Lisa Liswood Putman, Janet Daniels, Jennefer Atkins, Jane Nearing, Jessica Conniff, Maria Ey. Luihn, Lin Carvell, leedyc, Michelle, KLH, Lee MacClellan, philbog, Kelly Cummings, Deamiter, Josh Meneely, Liz Cormier, Claudia Field, Betsy Perry, Mary Kearney, Katrina Hunt, Marie DiBart, Doug Jackson, Kirsten Chervinsky, Penny Shima Glanz, Heather Vance, Tamara Johnston, Lizzie White, Vickie Selleck, Nina Rynearson, Janice Hopper, W.E. Gorlick, Jennifer, Joy Jakubaitis, Michelle Daimer, Marie Irshad, Concetta Phillipps, Megan Larsen, Veronica Svatos DeLuca, Saffron Williams, Chris, Linda Swartwout, Elly Doyle, Guido Stein, Emily Thayer, Rie Langdon, Gloria Shankle, Jennifer Vancalcar, Mary Anne Sedney, Joanne Burrows, Susanne Creativemother, Shael Hawman, Deirdre, Sharon Perez Patrick, Nathania Apple, Heather Welsh, Nina, Linda Randall, Laurine Gilbert, Lise Brackbill, Susan Poulter, Audrey mcelravy, sojourner, AuroraLee, Alexander the Drake, Holly Easley, Edy Marlatt, Amy T, Anna Kidd, Amy Duncan, Beth Graham, James Turnbull, Lydia Ngo, Kathleen Pascuzzi, Allyson Dykhulzen & Ellyn Shannon.

Road sign in Fife, Scotland

| GIBLISTON | $1\frac{1}{2}$ | LOCHTY | $2\frac{1}{4}$ |
| LATHALLAN | $3\frac{1}{2}$ | HIGHAM | 4 |
| LARGOWARD | $4\frac{1}{2}$ | PEAT INN | $5\frac{1}{4}$ |
| GILSTON | $5\frac{1}{2}$ | CUPAR | 12 |
| MONTRAVE | 10 | ST ANDREWS | $9\frac{1}{2}$ |